Yes to the 7 Laws of A Glorious Marriage

By Vicky Roger

Yes to the 7 Laws of a Glorious Marriage
by Vicky Roger

Printed in the United States of America

ISBN 9781624199769

www.xulonpress.com

To Him who loves us
and has freed us
from our sins by His blood,
and who made us a kingdom,
priests to His God and Father—
to Him be glory and dominion
for ever and ever!
Amen
(Rev1:5-6 ESV)

"You are worthy, our Lord and God,
to receive glory and honor and power,
for You created all things,
and by Your will they were created
and have their being."
(Rev4:11)

Acknowledgements

Special Thanks to

Pastor Darrel Baer
Pastor Rob Goodman
Bill Finch
Jim Schumacher

For their precious insights in this book.

Our deep gratitude to:

Our late beloved Mentor, Prof. Z. T. Fomum, for his great input into our lives.

The Haggai Institute (HI) Worldwide, especially Dr Daniel Shu and HI-Cameroon for teaching us Christian Leadership, and how to format our teachings & seminars.

Prof. J. T. Mbafor, Pastor of the CMFI-Yaoundé Church, where we grew in the Lord.

Madeleine Yombi, and the World Conquest Music Team that led us to the Lord.

Pastor Robinson Fondong, and all the CMFI-Maryland brethren (Westminster and Riverdale), for teachings, encouragements, prayers, and other spiritual jewels.

Annette and Denis Williamson, for their amazing contribution.

Special Mention and thanksgivings for Groups and Churches who helped refine this teaching by organizing our Marriage Seminars:

Dr Leandre Kwawou, head Pastor, CMFI-Johannesburg, South Africa., first ever to receive this Ministry, and whom the Lord used to trigger this whole teaching concept.

Pastor Philip Kuruvila, Suzie & Samuel Nchinda, Church for the Nations, Geneva, Switzerland.

Simplice Takeu Ndago and the Cameroonian Association of Hamburg, Germany.

Pastor Albert Kongo, Linda and Audebert Tchinkou, CMFI-Paris, France.

Pastor Albert Leclercq, Marc and Cathy Batha, Apostolic Church, Brussels, Belgium;

Reverend Boureima Kimso, Niger Bethel Church, Niamey, Niger.

Pastor Emmanuel and Rosine Defo, CMFI-Manchester, UK.

Pastor Philip and Ruth Dassi, CMFI-London, UK.

Pastor Calvin Wuntcha, CMFI-Montreal Canada.

Ministers Salvador and Monique Ngalle Houston, Tx, USA.

Professor Victor Mbarika, Director, ICITD, Baton Rouge, LA, USA.

Pastor Serge Sefekme, House of Prayer and Victory Church, Ashburn, VA, USA.

Pastor Moise Wang, God Is King Center, Beltsville, MD, USA.

I am Vicky, the bride;
I am Roger, the man ;
And in 1993, the two became one:

VICKY ROGER

OUR TESTIMONY:

Six months after our marriage, a group of Born Again Christians came to our music studio to record an evangelistic album.

Until then, we considered ourselves to be Christians, yet living according to all the ways of this age, with the usual load of lies, deceit, immorality, covetousness, and so forth; we then believed that, as long as our good deeds outweighed our sins every day, God was ok with us; therefore we sincerely believed that we were true heaven-bound Christians.

So one can imagine the shock when, at the end of those recording sessions, two things happened:

-For the first time in our lives we had witnessed 15 people live for 11 days according to the purest biblical standards: no lies, no gossip, no slandering, no murmuring, no bad attitudes, and no act of rebellion. Only holy, good attitudes filled with prayers for each other, mutual respect and Christian love!

-Having heard the true Gospel of Jesus-Christ (through listening to the album), we clearly understood that at that point we were by no means saved, by biblical standards.

Therefore, we both repented of our sins, received Jesus as our Lord and Savior, and everything turned around for the best, as our Christian life journey began.

This book is the fruit of that amazing trip.
All along, the greatest revelation of all, for us, was:

"The Two shall become One"

And what better place to make that golden proclamation than in the blending of the authors' names?

Vicky Roger

FOREWORD

Delightful and happy families are becoming rarer in our North American culture. It is especially helpful to read current teaching on the committed work of developing happy and fulfilling marriages.

Too often couples unite in marriage with the fantasy that some magic wand will bring all the happiness and unity that they could ever dream of. Vicky and Roger have captured both the joy and the work of a successful marriage in this helpful book.

For those of us who have been married for a lengthy period of time, we understand clearly that the satisfaction and joy of marriage comes from the journey. The journey includes both success and failure, receiving and giving of love and forgiveness, as well as surprises of joy and love.

The lessons in this book are practical and helpful, primarily, because they come from the authors' own life experience. Their emphasis on applying Biblical principles to our relationships with our life companions brings authenticity to their teachings.

Biblical principles are not unique to some, but apply to all couples and life situations. The teachings in this book are useful for all cultures, ethnic origins, or economic settings.

This book could be quite useful in a variety of settings. Pastors could make good use of this work in pre-marital, post-marital, or crises counseling settings. Congregations could use it as a text for Sunday School or small group teaching. Couples could be encouraged to work through the book together on their own initiative or by checking in on mentors along the way. Pastors and couples could be quite creative in ways to make the best use of this helpful book.

The lessons in this book are not secrets. They are time-tested practices of marriage that work. These lessons are not magical short-cuts. They are principles and practices that become habits in successful and happy marriages. The wonderful hope of this book is that any of us can learn these lessons.

Happy marriages and peaceful lives are God's perfect hope for us all.

Darrell Baer
Conference Minister,
Franklin Mennonite Conference

RECOMMENDATION

ୠ

In every book, filters the life and experiences of the authors. This one by Vicky & Roger is a practical workbook spiced by their numerous testimonies. It will help every couple to strike the original match and become a model for their children and subsequent generations. Do not read this book except you really want the Divine Hand to remodel your marriage to what it was meant to be, and what can be more fulfilling than that?

I have known Vicky and Roger for more than ten years. They are a daily honeymoon couple and have been used of God through their seminars in Africa, America and beyond to open a new page for a blissful marriage in many homes. Yours would certainly not be an exception if you read this book with a mind to change.

Dr Daniel SHU
Regional Director, Haggai Institute Francophone Africa.
University Marriage Lecturer & Counselor.

THE STARTING POINT

VICKY ROGER

ℬ

At 2:00 PM on that Saturday morning of April 1994, as promised on the program flier, Pastor "JTM" concluded his special Marriage Retreat by insisting:

-I strongly recommend that each couple take a two-day fast next week, after which you should write to your spouse a love letter containing the complete list of all the things you don't like in him or her.

Please make sure you write that letter prayerfully and only after fasting, in order to avoid making it a carnal matter. The two of you should fast simultaneously and break the fast only after praying together. During that prayer session, each of you should hand your love letter to your spouse.

Please, do not argue over any of your spouse's reproaches. There is no one reason why the reproach could be untrue. If your spouse can see it, how much more so God, who can see deep into your heart and soul what no man can see?

> Besides, if your spouse declares that those things hurt, it has to be a reality; so just own up to it and do the right thing:
> Simply repent over those things which have hurt your family and marriage, and endeavor to cooperate with the Lord to change the situation.

Little did any of us know that by those very words he had just launched our Marriage Ministry!

We carried out his instructions to the letter. The next Thursday, after an intense hour of prayer, we met to hand each other the love letters, just before breaking our two-day fast.

But what a shock! We both fell from our personal pedestals of self-glory while discovering that both letters named at least 20 to 25 horrible traits of character that, for the record, were blatant to everyone else except ourselves, as we both were blinded by our respective egos.

Coming together after a session of serious fasting and prayer, the Spirit of the Lord had prepared us and softened our hearts, and we were ready.

We simply repented to each other, promising to change, God being our helper!

The next day, during our daily morning family prayer, we extended the restitution to our kids, each of us repenting over those items from those lists which had affected them and the whole family.

Bottom line: it all began with a desire to change!

INTRODUCTION 1

CHANGE IS NOT OPTIONAL, CHANGE IS A MUST!

There is this story of four near-blind people, who one day were brought close to an elephant:
one stood at its tail, one by its legs, one at its horn, and one by its ear.
All of them were asked one question:

"In one word, can you describe an elephant?"

Since they could not really see, the one who was at the tail saw this thing moving like a snake and declared:

"An elephant is a viper."

The second who was by the legs touched one, and

feeling a tough, rough and circular surface, logically said:

"An elephant is a trunk of some tree."

The third one at the horn looked at this big, long thing twisting like a constrictor, and he simply said:

"An elephant is an anaconda."

The one who was by the ear looked at this large leaf-looking thing like a Nenuphar and just announced:

"Hey, an elephant is a water lily leaf!"

All of them had serious grounds to proclaim whatever they thought an elephant to be, but we all know that an elephant is neither a viper, nor the trunk of a tree, nor an anaconda, nor a Water lily leaf.

Yet, each of them was really convinced that he saw the right thing, to the best of his knowledge.

In the case above, when you step back far enough to see the totality of the elephant, you realize that each of them saw only a little piece of an elephant.

Yet again, each of them had a legitimate ground for saying whatever he said an elephant was!

It goes the same way with marriage!

Could it be that many couples have problems, each fighting to demonstrate that marriage is a "snake" while the other calls it a "Water lily leaf" or an "anaconda"? Could it be that many couples spend time not seeing marriage the way it should be seen?

The reality is: Many people don't see marriage the way the Creator of marriage saw it.

And in many a couple, each person is trying to make his own point of view prevail, to "sell" his personal vision of marriage. And yet, if both could step back far enough just like in the case of the elephant, to truly see what marriage was supposed to be, then, things change.

The goal of this chapter is first to help all couples worldwide, whenever they have a problem, to just ask themselves a simple question:

"What if?"

"What if I don't see the whole picture?"

In other words, the first statement we want to make here is that marriage is, par excellence, the place for change. This is a place where each person in a couple has to yield, to accept the other's viewpoint, to question all the certitudes that he/she had, coming into the marriage, just saying in every situation:

"What if?"

THE REAL CHANGE: WHAT IF?

But how do you bring about change? Joel Barker has done a wonderful job with his paradigm shift videos seen worldwide, bringing incredible insights as to the why, the how, and deadly danger awaiting leaders who reject change in the name of:

"I've always done it this way, and it's been working so far for me, so why change?"

And what more than marriage symbolizes leadership?

To paraphrase the above, in other words, the perfect marriage killer is the approach:

"This is the way I am... many people before you have told me time and time again that I'm a terrific person just as I am, so sweetheart, if you truly love me, just adjust to me... I'm not changing."

We humbly suggest: Au contraire, change is a must!

Many reasons:

All specialists in human behavior agree that each of us is constantly changing his own world view with age, from teenage, through the early adult life in the twenties, the thirties, the forties, the famous half-century mark, to finally the senior age beyond the sixties.

This makes marriage a permanent "work in progress", since the initial deal of "I love you just the way you are" can go on only for so long, and since each of the two spouses constantly has to adjust to the changes undergoing, first in himself/herself, then in the other.

Thirdly, experience proves that, no matter how long a couple drags out the "fiancé – fiancée" period to "better know each other," the relationship changes after the official "yes" followed by the exchange of vows, rings and the signed marriage contract.

Finally, experience proves that, no matter how honest and true to each other a couple is during the "fiancé – fiancée" period, the actual marriage means "Showtime!" or "game on!"

Why?

There are—and always will be—things that the two hide from each other; or, to put it in a more romantic way, there are things they will discover about each other only after they get married, for various reasons:

-Calculated behavior versus spontaneity: Most dates during the engagement are somehow a series of prepared 'rendez-vous', as compared to the impromptu moments of catching each other off-guard in the intimacy of marriage.

-There will be normal things or behaviors to be discovered only as the new common life goes on.

-The way and the pace at which each adjusts from life as a single to life of a couple, as some previous habits will be "dragging their feet" into the newlywed life.

-Most couples are "coached" into marriage by parents, various counselors, or Church leaders, and just like in any coaching, there are always "game time" contingencies that the player must face on his/her own and for which personal judgment and adjustment are necessary.

-Sometimes, simply put, eyes are at last opened to face reality, which probably gave grounds for the famous, silly, wicked and oh-so-hated Italian proverb:

"Love makes you blind;
marriage restores your sight."

SO HOW DO YOU REALLY CHANGE?

Each of us functions as shown in the above illustration:

Our world view is the root for any durable change; that world view induces our beliefs, that generate our values, which in turn induce our attitudes. Our attitude provokes our behavior, and our behavior commands our actions.

Why did we symbolize change as a tree?

We once tried to destroy one branch of some tree which had grown toward our home in order to eliminate the danger of the branch penetrating our home and the possibility of a poisonous snake gaining access. So we cut off the branch.

Twelve months later, the branch had grown back completely and was now threatening to penetrate a window on the second floor. So we had to readdress the threat and this time, destroy the whole tree from the roots so as to completely eliminate the danger.

What are we saying?

Many people, just like in this experience, want to bring about change through a partial approach: by just changing their actions, changing their behavior, changing their attitudes; or even changing their values.

But, just as in the case of the tree, unless the change comes from the roots of your world view—from the way you look at the whole picture—every other change is just temporary, just like the branch that grows back and becomes even worse.

With inroads remaining to outside influences, many people don't succeed in change, or whenever they do change, it's just for a while.

Therefore, this is the reason why throughout this book, we will constantly refer to what we call "the root change" meaning, the world view change. This is so that if you can really grasp the new vision, then your change will be permanent—and you and your marriage will never be the same.

In our case, we got married in January 1993 and like most marriages, our debut was a constant clash of two personalities trying to fit together, in spite of the deep love we had for each other, and the profound conviction that each of us had made the perfect choice.

The breakthrough occurred in that marriage retreat organized by Joe T. M. our Pastor where, humbled in our inmost beings, we were confronted with the fact that indeed—like anything else—marriage has its own laws. And when, with time, those laws were revealed to us one by one by the One who is the Author of Marriage, we found that we had broken just about all of them, day in and day out.

We were brought to apply the same simple, pragmatic logic to solving our marital problems as one applied, say, to any broken equipment in our home.

As an example, what happens if you flip a light switch on and there's no light?
You typically proceed by elimination to find the problem:

> Is the bulb burnt-out? If NO, then...
> Is there a general power failure also affecting the neighboring houses? If NO, then...
> Is the breaker tripped or the fuse blown?
> If NO, then...
> Is the meter broken? If NO, then...
> Is this house zone experiencing a problem? If NO, then...
> Is the plug itself damaged? If NO, then...
> What about the wire? Damaged?

Most of the time, one or a combination of the steps above will help to identify the exact spot where the problem lies, and the solution therefore is found.

One might think this approach sounds too simple for something as complex as a marriage relationship. Nevertheless, it has worked so well for us and numerous other couples we've been privileged to share our experience with through special marriage seminars worldwide: From Niamey in Niger to Lansing, Michigan USA, as well as Paris, Brussels, and many other cities!

Dear reader, our number one goal is to bring about a permanent change for the best in your whole world view of marriage, hoping this book will become every couple's "troubleshooting" check-list when problems arise and an inspirational guide to greater heights when things go right.

The solemn "Yes" vowed on that memorable day will then convert into a "Yes" to Marriage Law No.1, "Yes" to Marriage Law No.2, on up to Law No.7, or simply put: Yes to the 7 Laws of a Glorious Marriage.

Remember, it all begins, in every situation, by the capacity to ask yourself a simple question:

"What if?"

INTRODUCTION 2

THE CENTRALITY OF MARRIAGE

As an introduction to the things yet to come, this may sound to some as if we were rediscovering hot water in the 21st century:

Marriage is the center of life.

In fact, Family is the center of life, and since Marriage is the Center of the family,

Marriage is the center of any life.

From the start, marriage/family is the center of the very concept of society itself!

THE CENTRALITY OF MARRIAGE IN THE SOCIETY

It is an established historic fact that the fall of every great civilization in the past has begun with the deterioration of the traditional family set-up; that is, father and mother (man and woman) raising their children according to the existing social morality.

The US Department of Justice's 2006 National Report proves with hard-cold facts and figures that:

A child living in a Father-Mother family set-up has up to 58% more chances never to get involved in such serious social issues as gangs, taking or selling drugs, running away from home, vandalism, and criminal assaults.

LIFE TIME JUVENILE DELINQUENCY

(Source: US Dept of Justice National Report, 2006) (*3)			
SOCIAL ISSUE	living with Mom and Dad	living in any other family configuration	difference
involved in gangs	5%	12%	58.33%
involved in marijuana	30%	40%	25%
involved in hard drugs	9%	13%	30.77%
involved in drugs sales	13%	19%	31.58%
run away from home	13%	25%	48%
vandalism	34%	41%	17.07%
criminal assault	20%	35%	42.86%

On the other hand, the US Department of Health and Human Services reports that:

"Researchers have found many benefits for children and youth who are raised by parents in healthy marriages, compared to unhealthy marriages, including the following" (*4):

More likely to attend college
More likely to succeed academically
Physically healthier
Emotionally healthier
Less likely to attempt or commit suicide
Demonstrate fewer behavioral problems in school
Less likely to be a victim of physical or sexual abuse
Less likely to abuse drugs or alcohol
Less likely to commit delinquent behaviors
Have a better relationship with their mothers and fathers
Decreases their chances of divorcing when they get married
Less likely to become pregnant as a teenager, or Impregnate someone.
Less likely to be sexually active as teenagers
Less likely to contract STD's
Less likely to be raised in poverty.

And today in the modern western society, it's so obvious that the "traditional" family configuration, that is, Father and Mother (Man and Woman) raising their children in a family home, is slowly but surely yielding to other configurations, which have proven for centuries to be guaranteed doom for the future of any society.

So, how do you get there?

THE GREAT DEVIATION

In the beginning, in every successful civilization throughout the ages, every man is raised to later get married, and be founder of his own family; his marriage and family are at the center of his life and motivations.

The first question in his mind is generally: how do I feed my family?

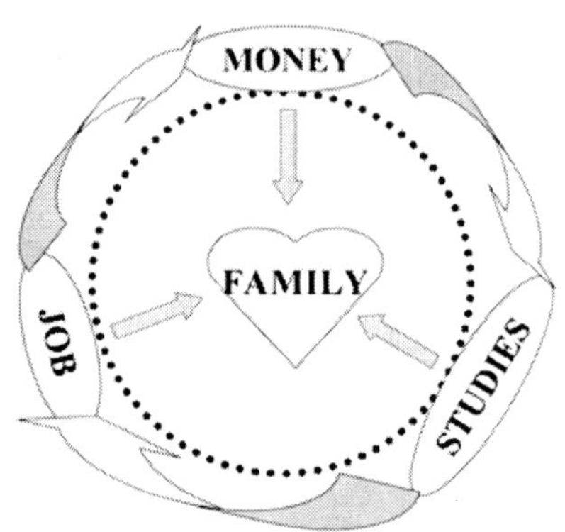

Answer: I need money with the goal to take care of my family.

Next question: how do I get money?

Answer: Get a job, to get the money, to take care of my family.

Then another question: how do I get a good job? Answer: have some education or training, to get a good job, to have good money, to take care of my family!

Eventually he will invest his earnings into the education of his children to complete the same cycle when they grow-up.

In short, the family is central; everything is aimed at the welfare of the family!

But today, we are witnessing a great deviation:

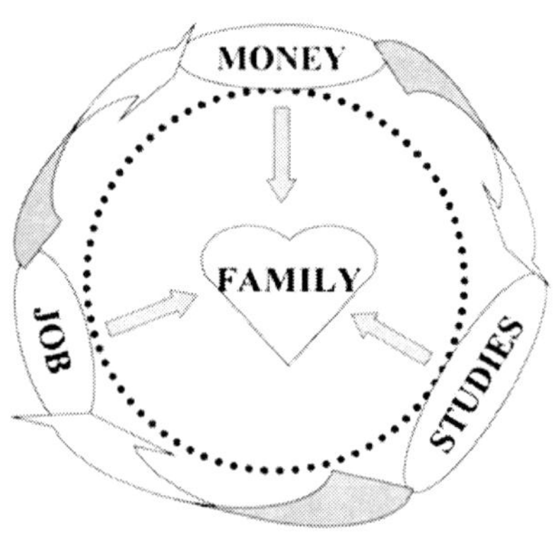

From centrality of family...

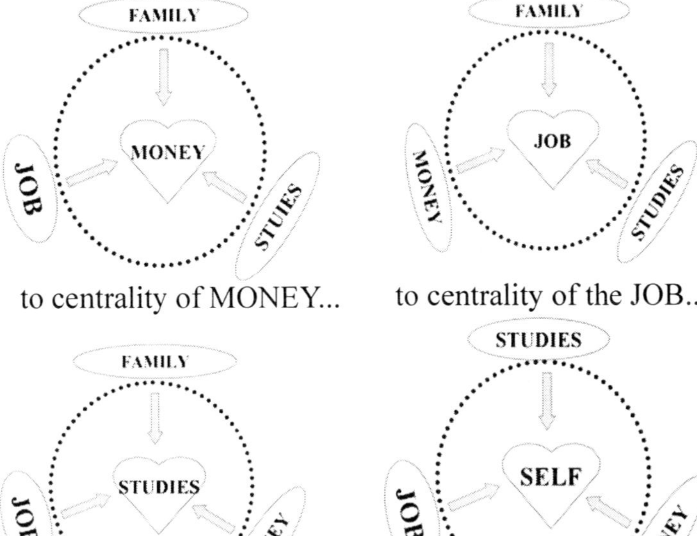

to centrality of MONEY... to centrality of the JOB...

to centrality of STUDIES! In many cases, the family is squarely removed from the picture, for the sole promotion of SELF.

It is believed that just after leading the Patriots to the final victory, the great hero, George Washington, was offered by his officers to lead his army in a "coup-d'état" aimed at using force to seize political power in the brand new United States of America just born out the ashes of a long, bloody and costly Revolution War against England.

It is said that after attempting to read the paper in front of him, Washington halted and, apparently very embarrassed, pulled out and donned his reading glasses which his officers had never seen on him before. Lifting his eyes to theirs, Washington simply said something like:

"I now need glasses to see, because this war has blinded me, just as it has blinded many of us..."

Meaning:

"How could we begin this Independence War with the great goal of ending England's dictatorship, and any form of dictatorship for this New World of ours still in the making, only to end up being ourselves dictators?

It is said that, like one man, all the audience burst into tears and that ended the matter!

In the same way, leaders of modern society should weep and weep, asking themselves the question:

How could we begin as a society, aiming at providing the best for our families, only to end up destroying the very notion of family, taking the family altogether out of the picture, once victory is at hand?

Dear reader, where do you stand in this big picture? Which among money, job, education, and self, has usurped the central place in your heart that belongs to the family alone?

Maybe this could be the starting point for a victory return… for all of us!

Unfortunately, this great deviation is not limited to the World, it concerns also many Christians, and we want to say it loud and clear:

The centrality of the family is in the perfect plan of God for humanity!

THE CENTRALITY OF THE MARRIAGE/FAMILY IN GOD'S PLAN FOR HUMANITY

Throughout the Bible, God has marriages/families in the very heart of His plans for humans:

Adam and Eve (Gen 1:27-28)

The very first thing God did when making Man was to create him as Man and Woman, and to immediately establish them as a family with the very purpose of raising children to do the same (we shall develop this further in a later chapter).

Noah (Gen 6-7)

Noah was the only one righteous in the eyes of the Lord, yet God could not save him alone and so made sure his whole family, that is, his wife alongside his three sons each with his wife, were all saved as well.

Abraham (Gen12:1-3)

The most amazing thing is when the Lord called Abraham in Genesis:

..."Get out of your country, from your family and from your father's house, to a land that I will show you. I will make you a great nation; I will bless you and make your name great; and you shall be a blessing. I will bless those who bless you, and I will curse him who curses you; <u>and in you all the families of the earth shall be blessed</u>."

(New KJV)

God's Master Plan for mankind was to be accomplished <u>through families</u> and <u>for families</u>. He planned from the start:

-To separate Abraham from his old pagan family;
-To create for him a new family;
-To use his family to bless all the families on Earth.

Lot (Gen 19:12-17)

Just like Noah, Lot was given a chance to save his entire family including his two sons-in-law, who yet had their chance, in spite of the fact they were citizens of Sodom and Gomorrah, which the Lord had decided to destroy by fire.

Rahab the prostitute from Jericho (Josh 2)

When given a chance to save herself from destruction, the deal was:

"This oath you made us swear will not be binding on us unless, when we enter the land, you have tied this scarlet cord in the window through which you let us down, and unless you have brought your father and mother, your brothers and all your family into your house."

The deal was respected during the actual destruction of the Jericho (Josh 6:25)

Moses

His childhood

We have always marveled at God's miracles to keep Moses from being killed while Pharaoh had ordered the annihilation of all Hebrew male newborn (Gen 1:25).

The amazing thing is that, in his miraculous ways, the Lord made sure that Moses 1) not only was spared, 2) but also adopted by Pharaoh's own daughter, 3) who decided to entrust him to an indentured Hebrew woman to breastfeed and raise him...4)…as counseled by a little 12-year-old Hebrew slave girl (the miracle of a queen taking the advice of an unknown person, let alone a slave girl!); 5) of all the potential mothers among the indentured women of Egypt, God made sure Moses ended up being raised by… his own natural mother and family! (Ex 2:1-8)

His ministry organization

First, God appointed Aaron, his own brother as his main co-minister (Ex 4:14), and Miriam, his sister, led the women in song and dance before the Lord as Israel rejoiced (Ex 15:20).

Secondly, from Exodus 32 throughout Numbers 10, under the direct orders from the Lord Himself, all the spiritual and social organization was laid upon families:

Priests and all spiritual ministries before the Lord were distributed according to families;

Military order of deployment was per families;

In fact, families are the mark of identity throughout the Old Testament (son of…).

Jesus (Matt 1:1-6)

Isn't it amazing how the New Testament begins with the Genealogy of Jesus-Christ?

It is as if the Lord is reminding everyone that Jesus:

> Who is the fulfillment of all the promises of God to Humanity (2 Cor 1:20);
> Who is the Savior (Luke 1:73);
> Who is the Messiah (Acts 2:36);
> Who is the promised Son of the Woman to crush the head of the Serpent of old, that is, Satan (Gen 3:15), to set men free from the bondage of sin (Matt 1:21);
> Who is the Ladder between Heaven and Earth unto salvation (John 1:51),
> to fulfill a prophecy given by God to Jacob more than 1,500 years ago (Gen 28:12);

that this Jesus has a family of His own, including all families on Earth: That is, the physical origins of your own family, whatever they may be, are represented in Jesus' own family: (As a matter of fact, His genealogy is extended to Adam in Luke 3:23-38 to include all humans).

Also that, whatever sin is hovering over and blocking your family, Jesus Himself has His own share of it in His own family!

Just follow His genealogy:

Abraham was an idol worshipper, from an idol worshipping family, when God called him to serve the only true God (Gen 12).

The same **Abraham**, when he had to go to Egypt after famine broke out, not only lied to Pharaoh that Sarah was his sister, but became rich out of that lie, and out of the fact that his wife had been given to Pharaoh (Gen 12:12-20).

His son **Isaac** was set to do the same in his own time, and only God saved his wife from disgrace (Gen 26:7-10).

Jacob was reputed to be a shrewd deceiver and even stole the blessing of his brother, Esau, from Isaac's mouth (Gen 27:30-37).

Judah committed incest and the Bible insists in Matthew 1:3 to remind everyone that his sons Perez and Zerah were born by Tamar, his daughter-in-law (Gen 38:12-26).

A few generations later, the Bible insists again (Matt 1:5) on the fact that **Boaz**, the son of **Salmon**, was born by Rahab, who happened to be that prostitute from Jericho (Josh 2:1).

The same **Boaz** begot his son **Obed**, King David's grandfather by Ruth, says the Scriptures, as if to remind us that Ruth was a Moabite, thus a descendant of Lot though yet another incest (Gen 19:36-38).

And finally the Scripture takes the time to reveal the

truth that **King Solomon**, among the family ancestors of Jesus-Christ, was son of **David by the wife of Uriah**; it does not even give the mother's name (Bathsheba), as if the Lord wanted through the inspiration of His Scriptures to remind everyone: Do not forget that David begot Solomon

-committing adultery with Uriah's wife,

-then killing the husband in an attempt to cover his sin.

Question: Why did the Bible, written Word of God under the inspiration of the Holy Spirit, not only expose these "embarrassing" details about Jesus' ancestry, but actually included them in the opening passages of the New Testament, the New Covenant, as the first step in the story of the most important person in the history of Mankind, Jesus-Christ, God Himself visiting his people? (Matt 1:23)

Why?

Answer: To remind everyone that This Jesus is indeed the fulfillment of God's promise to all families of the Earth, excepting none, no matter how terrible your family's sins are, no matter how shameful your family's past is.

It's as if Jesus is saying to humans:

"Have you got…

…idol worship in your family? So do I! Just look at my ancestors; Abraham and Solomon (1 Kings 11:4-9)!

…lying in your family? So do I! Just look at my ancestors Abraham and Jacob!

…incest in your family? So do I! Just look at my ancestors Judah and Ruth!

…prostitution in your family? So do I! Just look at my ancestor Rahab!

…cheaters in your family? So do I! Just look at my ancestor Jacob!

…murderers and adulterers in your family? So do I! Just look at my ancestor David!

...slaves in your family? My ancestors were slaves in Egypt, and after the Deportation for 70 years!"

It's as if Jesus is saying:
"Whatever ugly secret you have in your family, I have it in mine too; except, mine is out in the open in time and eternity for everybody to read; so just bring it on, I am the fulfillment of Abraham's blessings for all families on Earth, I am the Savior! And the Grace of God through me, Jesus-Christ, is extended to you too!!"

When you read the circumstances of His birth, it's as if Jesus continues saying:

"No matter how lowly the condition of your own family is, at least you were born among humans, on a human bed; see, I am the King of kings, yet I was born in a manger among beasts (Luke 2:7), so I can relate to you no matter who you are; just bring it on, I am the fulfillment of Abraham's blessings for all families on Earth, I am the Savior! And the Grace of God through me, Jesus-Christ, is extended to you too!!

"Come to me, all of you who are weary and carry heavy burdens, and I will give you rest" (Luke 11:28).

What an amazing grace!! Glory be to God!!

House Churches

As if it were to confirm God's interest in families as the primary target for Abraham's blessings extended to mankind, the early Church grew by the multiplication of House Churches, which were essentially households believing and turning each of their homes into a place to worship the Living God! Most of the time, the heads of the families became themselves the spiritual leaders of those house Churches (Acts 16:15; Rom 16:5; 1 Cor16:19; Phil 4:22; Col 4:15).

Amazingly, today's Church growth specialists all agree that the most effective way to achieve and sustain Church growth is through the same old concept of house Churches, which is ultimately re-establishing the family at the center of God's work, where it belongs:

Believe in Jesus and you'll be saved,
you and your household (Acts 16:31).

This is a sure promise of the Bible!

In the Bible, God has always extended His salvation to the entire family or household of the person rescued from a given situation. Family is so central in God's eyes that failure in this area is not an option; many just don't know it, and realize it…too late!!!

1Timothy 3:5 states:

(for if a man does not know how to rule his own house, how will he take care of the Church of God?);

Then in 1Timothy 5:8 the Scriptures continue:

Anyone who does not provide for their relatives,
and especially for their own household,
has denied the faith and is worse than an unbeliever.

The Bible is very clear: if you fail there, you could be "doing great things for God" all right, but that's in the human's eyes! As Apostle Paul said :

Now if anyone builds on this foundation with gold, silver, precious stones, wood, hay, straw, each one's work will become clear; for the Day will declare it, because it will be revealed by fire; and the fire will test each one's work, of what sort it is. (1 Cor3:12-13)

The above diagram can therefore be completed as seen here:

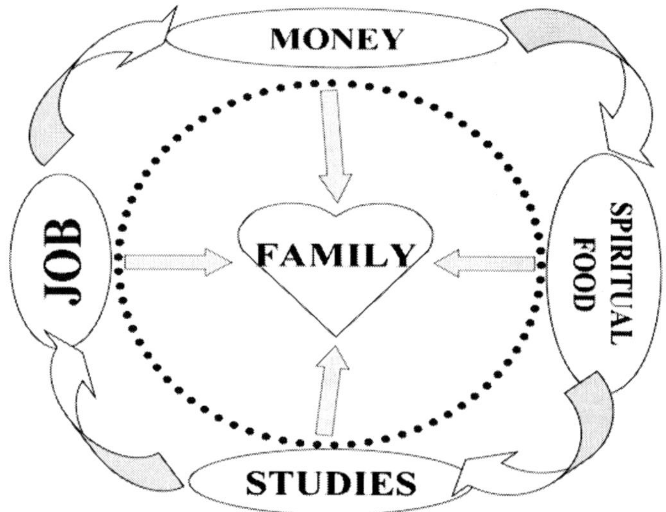

Therefore the great deviation might well include the spiritual aspect:

The final goal of your spirituality should be to provide spiritual food (as well as physical food) for your family (and we insist on the term "final goal", obviously, taking in account all the necessary periods of isolation for spiritual growth and those dictated by one's personal walk with the Lord).

Except for a person specifically called by the Lord to do otherwise, if your "spirituality" becomes central in your life, to the point of having your family (or marriage) become a satellite, chances are you are undergoing a deviation as well as the one who does it for his possessions, job, education or other social status.

And so, we can say that:

The centrality of the family is not negotiable, it is the center of human life itself.

CHRISTIAN MARRIAGES ARE THE N° 1 TARGET OF THE ENEMY

It is well documented that, a few years back, one hundred witch doctors from South Africa together took a 40-day fast, with only one goal: destroy Christian marriages (*6).

If you still had any doubt about the centrality of marriage in the life of Christians, just ask yourself one question: why is it that Christian marriages are the N°1 target of the enemy against God's Church?

The answer is evident: because, being very knowledgeable of the Scriptures (Matt 4:5), the devil knows very well that once a believer's marriage has failed, any other service to the Lord is just a big noise, with no eternal impact in the Kingdom of God (1 Tim3:5, 1 Cor 13:1).

Root question: Is Marriage/Family central in your World view?

Is there anything, like career, financial or material property, self-promotion item, etc., personal spiritual goals included, for which you are ready to jeopardize your marriage/family?

If "yes", this is the root change that will turn things around for true blessings!

CHAPTER I

YES TO LAW N^{O}1: The Law of Manuals

VICKY ROGER

"We were about eight months in the Lord! One night, someone walked into our Music Studio and put his cup of coffee on the Main mixer; we kindly reminded him our golden rule: no food or beverages anywhere near the electronic instruments or equipment!

From that moment, the Holy Spirit began to ask us a simple question:

'How about your life? How about your marriage? Do you do the same for your life and for your marriage?"

And suddenly we just realized that, just like those musical instruments, Marriage was a Creation, having a Creator, who had provided a manual for it!
Long story short, we simply responded:

"Yes Lord, yes to establishing your Manual as the Guide for our Marriage"

Indeed, what we meant was: "Yes" to the Law of Manuals!

Our first "yes"!"

SO LOGICAL...
EXCEPT WITH THE MOST PRECIOUS

It's easy to see just how logical people are in everything they do. Take for example, the investments people routinely make such as:

Spending money to get a driver's license so one can drive according to the manual and the code for reasons of safety and protection for their car.

Paying to become well trained to use computers more efficiently.

Paying for training to use different equipments for jobs and in everyday life.

Whenever they acquire a new gadget or device:

They insist on getting the owner's manual for it.

They usually study the device and read up on it very thoroughly, or at the very least, get someone to explain to them the essential part of how it works. Most have an understanding of it before proceeding with the actual use of it.

They cautiously begin using the equipment step by step, while mindful of the manual's instructions for use.

They usually submit without question to the guidelines, and principally, they make sure not to violate any "WARNING", "CAUTION" or "ATTENTION" notice- such as those typically found in the first pages of any manual.

Whenever there is a problem, they go back to the "troubleshooting" section of the manual, or they seek assistance from a person who specializes in fixing that equipment.

They usually follow the instructions given to them carefully, and so on.

Yes, people are really very logical. However, the most amazing thing happens when it comes to life itself.

All this beautiful logic stops when it comes to the one and only most precious property each of us owns: Our body, our life.

The average person rarely says:

"Is there any manual for this wonderful, precious life of mine?"
"Is there a creator of my marriage?"
"What does the Creator of this thing think about it? How did He plan for it to work?"

Instead, many make their own rules.

YET THERE IS A CREATOR AND A MANUAL

The Bible says in Genesis 2:

But for Adam no suitable helper was found. So the LORD God caused the man to fall into a deep sleep; and while he was sleeping, he took one of the man's ribs and closed up the place with flesh. Then the LORD God made a woman from the rib he had taken out of the man, and he brought her to the man. The man said, "This is now bone of my bones and flesh of my flesh; she shall be called 'woman, for she was taken out of man.". then "...God blessed them and said to them, "Be fruitful and increase in number... "
(Gen 1:28)

This clearly states that God created marriage at a time when man had no idea about his own need.

Every good creation (cars, computers, programs, games, etc.) comes with a manual.

It's only logical that the One who created man gave us a manual for His own creation—man and woman—including how we relate to each other, particularly in marriage.

GOD IN YOUR MARRIAGE

Marriage was intended to be like a three-legged stool for it to stand. The first leg is the husband; the second leg is the wife; and the third leg should be God.

We say "should be" simply because the reality is that many couples try to just make their marriage work like a two-legged stool.

And we all know how unbalanced that proverbial two-legged stool would be—without even attempting to sit on one!

Could this be the first and main reason why the divorce toll has risen to record highs in the modern civilization, as biblical values are being more and more removed from our rules and laws, and therefore from our daily life?

What are we saying?
God should, by all means, be present in a marriage.
In our seminars, when we ask people:
"How do you bring God into the marriage?"
The usual answers are:
Prayer, Communion, Family prayer, Going to Church, Bringing up the children to know God, Sunday schools, Giving to God, Fasting, Reading the Bible, Meditating on and/or studying the Word of God, etc.
All these answers are excellent and should all be put to practice; we want to emphasize on two specific aspects from our own personal experience.

FAMILY PRAYER: A PLACE OF VICTORY.

First, praying together as a family and particularly as a couple: We have learned that it's crucially important for a couple to pray together every single day. In fact, we have made it a duty never to leave home without praying as a family because:

Praying together brings hearts together. Many very good books on prayer will confirm this, and we have personally verified that wonderful biblical truth to be totally authentic. On the other hand, prayer is the perfect place for reconciliation and healing relationships (Matt 5:23-24)

This is a place where God can manifest Himself to the whole family, to the children, and to the entire household as the true living, wonder-working God and the One who makes miracles.

We can't count how many critical situations we have had—where we just prayed as a family, crying out to God for a miracle—and every single time, the Faithful Lord has pulled us through.

These experiences have marked our children for life, because it is, par excellence, the unique place for them to see God at work, on a regular basis. In fact, every single child who has lived with us, whether for a short or a long period, has witnessed such wonders and most of them have grown to really love and fear the Lord.

Last but not least, in Exodus 17:8-13 the Bible says: *The Amalekites came and attacked the Israelites at Rephidim. Moses said to Joshua, "Choose some of our men and go out to fight the Amalekites. Tomorrow I will stand on top of the hill with the staff of God in my hands."*

So Joshua fought the Amalekites as Moses had ordered, and Moses, Aaron and Hur went to the top of the hill. 11 As long as Moses held up his hands, the Israelites were winning, but whenever he lowered his hands, the Amalekites were winning. 12 When Moses' hands grew tired, they took a stone and put it under him and he sat on it. Aaron and Hur held his hands up—one on one side, one on the other—so that his hands remained steady till sunset. 13 So Joshua overcame the Amalekite army with the sword.

The lesson is:
There are two dimensions to every battle:

First, the physical battle, that is, Joshua and the Army of Israel in the valley, stands for our daily life struggles at all levels: family, society, job, etc.

Then the spiritual one, symbolized by the staff of Moses, is our prayers, and other spiritual activities, lifted up to heaven in order to bring God to move into our daily situations and issues.

Victory depended, not on the skills of Joshua and his army, but on the lifting up of Moses' staff.

This passage states a spiritual law:

The mere act of lifting the spiritual staff (for example: your prayer, your fasting, your praise and worship as a family), establishes victory in the invisible; then all you have to do is walk into that victory in the visible.
Simply said:

Praying every morning as a family establishes victory in all your activities for the whole day.

Why deprive yourself and your family of such a precious asset?

USING THE MANUAL

REVISITING THE NOTION OF FAMILY PROVISION

Jesus said:
Man shall not live on bread alone, but on every word that comes from the mouth of God. (Matt4:4)

He was actually quoting what Moses said to the people of God in Deuteronomy 8:3:

For nearly 40 years, an estimated crowd of more than 3 million people were nourished in the desert with the manna, the perfect symbol of the "other provision" needed for a full life in God's eyes (it came straight from God's word, no other human effort was needed); the manna was to be dealt with, every day, this way:
And He orders you to gather about two quarts for each person in your family..."
Exodus 16:16 Contemporary English Version (CEV)

In other words:

In order to have a full life in the Lord's eyes, every human needs not only the physical food but also the spiritual food of the Word of God!

It is therefore your responsibility to provide not only the physical, but also the Spiritual food at your family table daily!

THE ONLY JUDGE

Another aspect of the use of the Manual is the fact that the Word of God should be present in the family as the final referee and judge of any problem.

For any given instrument in our possession, we

usually refer to the manual as the final authority for any issue; it is simply common sense to do the same for Marriage.

A PLACE OF REPENTANCE, NOT ACCUSATION

In the early times of our Christian life, we had issues almost every week as a couple. We sought help from our spiritual parents; and boy, we would go at it—each heaping as many accusations on the other as possible. No real lasting solution could be found until the Lord revealed to us this horrible truth:

Why are you playing the role of the Devil?
He is the accuser of God's children!

What a shock!

Jesus said:

"*Why do you look at the speck that is in your brother's eye, but do not notice the log that is in your own eye? Or how can you say to your brother, 'Let me take the speck out of your eye,' and behold, the log is in your own eye? You hypocrite, first take the log out of your own eye, and then you will see clearly to take the speck out of your brother's eye.*
(Matthew 7:3-5)

The Lord was simply stating that every time you look at somebody else's mistakes before acknowledging your own (and in this context, in the family for example), you are declaring:

"I am a hypocrite!"

In other words:

The Word of God is not a place of accusation,
but a place of repentance!

The truth is:

It takes two people to have a problem;

No matter how small your share is in causing that problem, that share needs to be removed to solve the issue.

If you and I have a problem, there is no lasting solution until the issue is out of my heart; and I am the only one who can remove it out of my heart, and vice versa.

In God's method a couple's problem is addressed this way:

-They acknowledge there is a problem.

-They go to the Manual, or Righteous referee, the Lord, through His Word.

-There, in the Bible they find the passage(s) addressing their problem— if they can't figure it out, a pastor or a spiritual counselor can help.

-In the light of the stated biblical truths, each acknowledges his/her own mistakes; repents to God and to the other; and thereby, removes from himself his own bad spots, and before you know it, there is no more problem on the table.

The Word of God in a family should be used as a mirror (James 1:23) in which each person, from parents to children looks at himself, and removes all the "dark spots" of his own soul which need to be cleansed as a result of a violation to this Word of God (Eph 5:26).

That's why it is important for families to read the Word of God, and for the children to be taught.

Parents should buy a Bible for each individual child just as they buy other school books and toys.

CLOSER TO GOD, CLOSER TO EACH OTHER

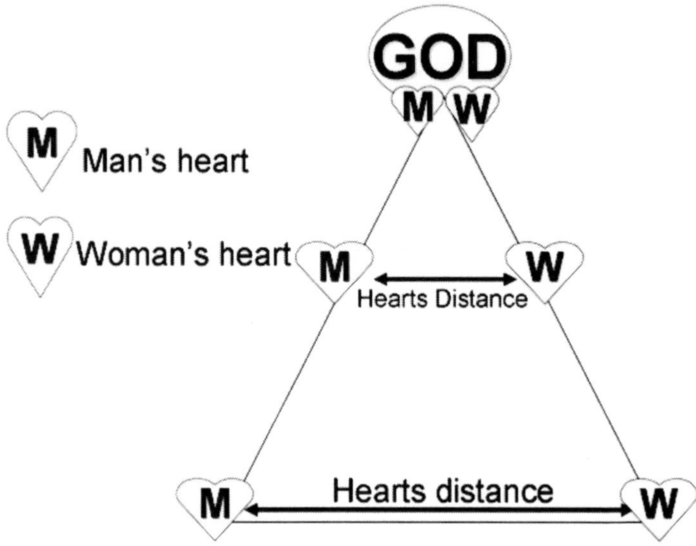

How do we put this? Harry, a brother in the Lord, blessed us with this wonderful visual explanation:

The closer the hearts of man and wife are to God,
the closer their hearts are together.

One day, when we were driving to Jessup, MD for one of our Marriage Seminars, we decided to sing praises to the Lord all the way there. We were in the front seats, while our daughter Chouchou was in the back.

Any one of us would just begin a song as led by the Spirit, and the rest would simply sing along freely. After about 25 minutes of praise and now fully connected with the Lord, a remarkable thing occurred not just once, but three times in a row! Both of us, without consulting the other, started up with exactly the same song after ending the previous one!

It was an amazing illustration of the "Heart Distance" diagram pictured above!

As our spirits were plugged to the fullest into God through our praise and worship, our hearts were so close to each other that we could sense and feel exactly the same thing!

In that seminar, we gave testimony of that experience to illustrate the diagram!

Praise to the Lord!!

SUMMARY

Yes to law No.1 means "Yes" to establishing God as the center of a marriage, through the usual spiritual activities recommended in every good Church; particularly :

Each family, babies included, should pray together every day; this alone welds hearts together in unity and establishes Victory in your daily activities.

As much as you need the daily bread to feed your family, it is also your duty to provide them with the spiritual bread of the Word of God for a full life.

Every one in the family should have his/her own Bible; this includes children!

Finally, the Word of God should be central and final for resolving issues, not a place of accusation, but rather a place of repentance where each person acknowledges his own shortcomings and spiritually removes his own sins; this is the Christian way to resolve problems, and the best way to resolve marital problems.

Root question: Do you find it "ok" to submit without conditions to the prescriptions in the manual for any of your instruments or equipments, and yet, to create your own rules when it comes to your most precious one, that is, your body, life and Marriage?

Root Change: You should go back to the Manual, and establish God as the Center of your marriage through His Word.

CHAPTER I I

YES TO LAW N°2: THE LAW OF CREATION

𝔄

THE LAW OF CREATION (Part A): PROCLAMATION

ROGER

𝔏

"I was eight years old then; the elder sister of a friend of mine, who was 4 years older than both of us, used to terrorize us. One day, after I rebelled against her tyranny, she just yelled at me:

"You...you...you will not love your wife!"

I immediately started to proclaim: *"Au contraire, Madame, I will the greatest husband to my wife!"*

I kept repeating it over and over, and over to myself for many days: *"I will the greatest husband to my wife!"*

Amazingly, three years later, while I was taking the exam to be admitted to high school, the examiner asked me the question: "Tell me three things you would love to become in the future."

My first answer was:

"I will be the greatest husband to my wife."

GOD GAVE YOU POWER TO CREATE THROUGH PROCLAMATIONS!

And God said, Let there be light; and there was light. And God saw that the light was good (suitable, pleasant) and He approved it; and God separated the light from the darkness. And God called the light Day, and the darkness He called Night. And there was evening and there was morning, one day. (Gen 1:3-5)

In Genesis Chapter 1, verses 1-26, for each step of the Creation, The Bible consistently says:
"God said... " And it just came to pass.
In Genesis 1:27 The Bible says:

" So God created man in His own image, in the image and likeness of God He created him; male and female He created them" (Amplified Bible)

This means that God created man to be like God and to function like God!

The first thing we want to say is that, as Don Gosset and Keening put it:

"The whole creation process
was a series of proclamations." (*5)

I*n the beginning was the Word, and the Word was with God, and the Word was God. 2 He was in the beginning with God. 3 All things were made through Him, and without Him nothing was made that was made.(John 1 :1-3)*

The Good News Is: God gave us, humans, His ability to create through every proclamation from our lips.

The Bad News Is: More often than not, we choose to proclaim (therefore create) doom and calamity.

Let us begin by dissecting Numbers 14:28:

"Tell them: as surely as I live, declares the Lord, I will do to you the very thing I heard you say."

In this passage, God was speaking to the people of Israel. Out of more than 603,500 people, only two (Caleb and Joshua) said :

"The land we passed through to spy out is an exceedingly good land. If the LORD delights in us, then He will bring us into this land and give it to us, ... Do not fear them." (Numbers 14:7-9)

All the rest said:

""We wish we had died in Egypt or somewhere out here in the desert!!...". (Numbers 14:2 CEV)

And that's exactly what happened. Each of them reaped the fruit of his own proclamation. Only Caleb and Joshua made it to the Promised Land, while the rest of the people (603,500+) died in the wilderness.

This is clearly a spiritual law which has been repeatedly confirmed through the Scriptures. Man was created just like God and was granted the capacity to create, to shape his own life and destiny through his proclamations.

In his excellent book, "A Successful Marriage: the Husband's Making" (*2) Professor Z. T. Fomum asked:

"Do you know that you are a prophet in your own home?"

Many couples proclaim so many things on each other particularly when things go wrong—or when they are angry!

Question: Did you know that in that process you are creating, shaping your spouse according to your proclamation?

In the long run, he or she will turn out to be exactly the fruit of your proclamations. Believe us, it is a spiritual law as sure and true as gravity is a physical reality!

Close your eyes for a second, and remember all the things you have been proclaiming on your spouse, on your children, on your business, on your family, on everything under your authority.

And now look at what they are. You will be stunned to see that they—wife, husband, children, etc.—are exactly what you proclaimed them to be.

In the excellent book, "The Power of Your Words" by Don Gosset and Keening (*5), this process is clearly explained. We paraphrase it as follows:

Whenever you proclaim a good thing, God takes the good thing and makes it a reality on you, on your wife, on your children, and whatever or whoever you proclaim that good thing upon.

Whenever you proclaim a bad thing, the devil, (who, contrary to man, was not created in the image and likeness of God) then takes whatever you proclaim. Not having the power to create, yet he has the power to transform a little spark into a major fire, to transform a little wind into a major storm.

So, whenever you proclaim something negative, the enemy will take it, blow it out of proportion and throw it back on your wife, your husband, your family, your business, or whatever or whoever is under your authority, to make it a huge and ugly reality.

Again, every proclamation of yours, particularly upon your family becomes a creation.

For good or bad, the choice is all up to you!

THE CREATING POWER OF WORDS IS SO CRUCIAL THAT AFTER THE INITIAL CREATION, EVERY IMPORTANT EVENT IN THE BIBLE HAD TO BE PROCLAIMED IN ADVANCE .

Throughout the Scriptures, proclamation (by men) is found in many forms:

Prayers or prophecies, names (their meaning) and direct proclamations. Let us scroll through The Bible, and see how the major steps of the journey of the people of God were proclaimed in advance:

The Flood

God chose Noah to be the prophet of the flood (Gen 6:13-22, 2 Pet 2 :5). On the other hand, his name was a prophetic proclamation in those times of total distress and wickedness meaning: " The one who will give mankind rest from their intense suffering." (Gen 5:29)

400 Year Slavery in Egypt

God Himself proclaimed that prophecy to Abraham more than 150 years before it happened (Gen 15:13-14).

Out of Egypt

Joseph proclaimed it more than 350 years in advance (Gen 50:24-25).

Promised Land

The Israelites were required by Moses to proclaim blessings and curses on the promised land prior to occupying it (Deut 27).

Deportation

Isaiah, Jeremiah, prophetess Huldah (2 Kings 22:14) and even Asaph (Ps 79) all proclaimed the destruction of Jerusalem and the deportation to Babylon, up to 400 years in advance.

The Return From Deportation

Jeremiah proclaimed its exact duration: 70 years (Jer 29:10, Ezra 1:1).

The Fall of Babylon

Jeremiah had written on a scroll about all the disasters to come upon Babylon (Jer 51:60-64). Jeremiah even sent Baruch to go to Babylon only to proclaim its fall.

The Advent of Jesus

More than 300 prophecies proclaimed in detail the advent, the birth through a virgin, the ministry, the betrayal by Judas, the death, the resurrection, the rising and the second coming of Jesus. Luke 2:25-38: Simon and Anna prayed (proclaimed) the Lord in.

THE CREATING POWER OF PROCLAMATION THROUGH NAMES IS SO EFFECTIVE THAT EVERY PERSON OF CONSEQUENCE IN GOD'S PLAN, EITHER HAD A NAME RELATING TO HIS MISSION, OR GOT A NAME CHANGE TO FIT THAT MISSION.

ADAM: Means Mankind.

EVE: Means the mother of all the living (Gen 3:20).

NOAH: Again, his name was a prophetic proclamation in those times of total distress and wickedness meaning: The one who will give Mankind rest from their intense suffering (Gen 5:29).

ABRAHAM: Originally, he was Abram, meaning exalted father but his name was changed to Abraham (or the father of many) to fulfill God's purpose (Gen 17:5):

"All families on earth will be blessed through you."
(Gen 12:3)

ISRAEL: He was originally called Jacob or deceiver (Gen 37:36), definitely not a name suited for any purpose of God. The Lord changed his name to Israel:

because you struggled with God and with men and won.
(Gen 32:28)

MOSES: His name means "saved from the water." Not only was he, himself, saved from the waters (Ex 1), but also he led the people of Israel to final salvation from Egyptians through the waters of the Red Sea.

JOSHUA: Moses changed his name from Hoshea (salvation) to Joshua (the Lord saves - Numbers 13:16). One amazing statistic illustrates this: Except for the 36 who fell because of Achan's sin (Josh 7), he led an army of more than 400,000 men in 13+ years of war without losing one single man (Numbers 31:49; Josh 8 to Josh 11; Jos 21:45)—only God could do this! The Lord was surely saving through him!

DAVID: means beloved. Just fits the man after God's heart!

SOLOMON: His name means Peaceful, says The Bible (1 Chronicles 22:9); and Solomon is the only king in The Bible who never had to worry about war.

JESUS: means Savior (Matt 1:21- Amplified Bible).

PETER: The Lord changed his name from Simon to Peter which means rock or stone, and He declared:

"... I tell you that you are Peter, and on this rock I will build my Church, and the gates of Hades will not overcome it." (Matt 16:18)

Jesus thereby was declaring Peter as the first stone of flesh in His new temple, the Body of Christ, as Peter himself expressed it later:

"*You also, like living stones, are being built into a spiritual house to be a holy priesthood, offering spiritual sacrifices acceptable to God through Jesus Christ." (1 Pet* 2:5)

PAUL: Initially called Saul, chose to be called Paul on the very first step of his first Mission trip; Paul actually was a roman name, Paulus, therefore identifying him with the Gentiles whose apostle he was, as he himself declared in Rom 1:1-5.

THE POWER OF PROPHETIC PROCLAMATION THROUGH NAMING: THE EXAMPLE OF THE SONS OF JACOB

One stunning illustration of this in the Bible is the names of the sons of Jacob (Gen 29 – Gen 31:30).

RUBEN: According to the French Bible "Parole Vivante", Ruben means: "People have seen my shame". And sure enough, when Ruben was old enough, he brought shame to his father by sleeping with his concubine. (Gen 35:22)

SIMEON: Meaning "I am not loved". Four things about Simeon:

When all the brethren of Joseph went to Egypt, one had to be put in prison while waiting for the remaining nine to come back. Guess who? Simeon: " I am not loved".

Through the entire Bible there is not one man of consequence, not one prophet, not one great person who's achieved anything of consequence for the kingdom of God coming out of the tribe of Simeon. Not one.

Third thing: When his father, Jacob, was blessing all his children, all he had to say about Simeon (Gen 49:6) was: "I *have no part with you.*" Some blessing!

Finally, in Deuteronomy 33, when Moses was blessing all the tribes of Israel, he actually forgot one tribe. Guess who? Simeon: "I am not loved".

LEVI: His name means "Attached to me" and sure enough, when the people had made the golden cow and Moses asked in Exodus 32:26:

"Whoever is for the Lord, let him come to me",

The Bible says that all the tribe of the Levites stood up to stay with the Lord. As a reward, the Lord attached them to Him to be His priests. "Attached to me". Prophecy fulfilled.

JUDAH: Means "the praise of the Lord". And where did the Savior, the Messiah, the Praise of the Lord, the Glory of the Lord come from? The tribe of Judah. Prophecy fulfilled.

BENJAMIN: Genesis 35:18: At his birth, his dying mother named him "Ben-Oni" meaning "Son of my bitterness". Later the father changed the name into "Benjamin" meaning "Son of my joy"; but the harm was done. And throughout The Bible, Benjamin has been always a source of joy, then bitterness, then joy, etc.

First, the Benjamites committed the double infamy of trying to sodomize a sojourner passing by and then secondly, they gang-raped his wife and killed her (Judges 19-25). As a result, the rest of the tribes almost wiped them out of Israel leaving only 600 men (Judges 20:47-48). That's bitterness! Then, feeling compassion for the survivors, they restored them, pampered them and even creatively provided them with virgin Israelite girls to be their wives–that's joy!

Second, the first king of Israel, Saul was from the

Benjamites, which is glorious Joy. The story eventually turned sour when Saul disobeyed God and was destituted as king, causing a civil war: Bitterness!

Paul the great apostle, the apostle of the gentiles was a Benjamite. But he started by killing believers: Bitterness! And at the end, he became the joy of the Gentiles, the joy of the Lord by being the apostle of the Gentiles, and the author of half of the books of the New Testament: Joy, bitterness, joy, bitterness, so it went with Benjamin. Prophecy fulfilled.

RACHEL – NABAL:

Yet one of the most striking examples of the power of proclamation is the tandem Rachel – Nabal. What do they have in common?

Rachel: In Genesis 31:32, Jacob was caught by Laban who was pursuing him; he carelessly said:

"Whoever has taken your gods, your idols shall not live"
(therefore "will die")

How could he imagine that Rachel, his beloved favorite wife, had taken the gods of Laban? Actually, he was pronouncing a death sentence with that proclamation.

She died some time later in the wilderness, while giving birth to Jacob's last son, Benjamin. (Gen 35:18)

Nabal: In 1Samuel 25 Abigail, the wife of Nabal said to David (1 Samuel 25:26):

"May your enemies and all who intend
to harm my master be like Nabal".

Then later, in verse 29, she added:

"but the lives of your enemies, God will hurl away as from the pocket of sling".

In other words, she associated the fate of Nabal to the fate of the enemies of David and proclaimed:

"May God just kill all of them".

The Bible says in verse 38 that ten days later, God struck Nabal and he died.

These are two examples of a husband who carelessly proclaims the death of his beloved wife and a man whose fate was determined by the proclamations of his wife.

Oh, the power of careless words in a family!

Again, there is a prophecy in every proclamation you make in your family, and there is a spiritual law stating:

"I (God) will do exactly according to what you say". (Numbers 14:28)

What kind of wife, husband, children, business, Ministry do you want? What kind of family do you want? It is up to you, right there in your lips.

"The tongue has the power of life and death and those who love it will eat its fruits." (Proverbs 18:21)

In 2005 we organized a Marriage Seminar in Niamey, Niger; the next day, a participant, who was a Bishop and National Chairman for his denomination, invited us for lunch.

There, he confided to us the following:

"After you shared on this creating power of proclamations, I got back home and could not sleep, realizing that all my family was exactly the fruit of my proclamations for the last 20 years or more, not good things at all! So I cried for mercy and forgiveness all night long before God.

At 4:00 in the morning, I woke up my wife and seven

children, knelt down before them and begged them to forgive me for the disaster I had caused by my negative proclamations over all of them!"

Root change:

Please acknowledge, and accept, and let it sink into your heart that by creating you in His image and likeness, God has given you a powerful piece of divinity—The capacity to create by a mere proclamation!

It is a frightening force right there, in the center of your face, on your lips and all you have to do is to choose life rather than death, choose to proclaim always the good and never the bad for your marriage, for your own life and for your family.

Choose to always project 20 years from now before any proclamation and just ask yourself:

Will I be proud of it,
when I reap the fruit of my proclamation?

HOW TO UNDO THE PAST NEGATIVE PROCLAMATIONS?

We strongly recommend that you read "The Power of Your Words" by Don Gosset and Keening, which has revolutionized our own marriage and life, then go through the usual pathway to true repentance:

-Own up to the fact that you have sinned by proclaiming negatives on yourself, your spouse, your life, your kids, your family, your business, or anyone under your authority.

-Make a complete list of all negative proclamations for each category.

-Confess them all to God and ask for forgiveness one by one.

-Before God, prayerfully annul them one by one, and

turn away from each of them, pledging never to return on that pathway again.

-Carry all necessary restitutions to anyone you have affected by your past negative proclamations.

HOW TO CHANGE?

After erasing the past, how do you destroy years and years of the bad habit of negative proclamations from your lips? The answer is simple: the same way you got there—practice, practice, practice!!

HOW TO BUILD POSITIVE PROCLAMATIONS?

After due restitution as prescribed above, make a list of positives you would like to see in every aspect of your life, spouse, marriage, family, business and ministry.

Do not hesitate to rename or change any name, nickname which is a negative proclamation, even if it means legal name change.

Train yourself daily to proclaim those positives.

In the same process, repent and correct immediately if an old bad habit slips into your lips to make you proclaim a negative.

Pray daily for the grace to destroy negative thinking from your heart (The Bible says the mouth speaks out of the abundance of the heart). Be alert to immediately erase and repent over any negative thought popping into your mind.

As much as possible, avoid bad companions who use the kind of vocabulary you are trying to erase from your mouth.

Pray that God give you the stamina never to quit this reverse training and grant you victory.

May the Lord bless you!!

ATTACK THE PROBLEM (OR THE SPIRIT BEHIND), DON'T ATTACK THE PERSON!

One question is raised in almost every single Seminar:

Since I cannot call my spouse bad names, for fear of bringing a curse on him/her through my proclamation, what do I do then, in order to address the issue?

Answer: WJWD (What Jesus Would Do)!

Just follow the Master:

When Peter opposed Him in an attempt to keep Him from the Cross, therefore from God's perfect, eternal Plan for Humanity, instead of:

"Peter, you are so carnal!"

Jesus said:

"Get behind me, Satan! You are a stumbling block to me; you do not have in mind the concerns of God, but merely human concerns. (Matt 16:23)

Lesson: He attacked the spirit behind.

When James and John requested to sit in His kingdom, one on His right hand and one on the other, causing indignation from the rest of the Twelve, instead of:

"James and John, you are so presumptuous and proud!"

Jesus said:

"You do not know what you ask".

Then He gave a teaching on how to aspire to Christian greatness: (Matt 20: 20-28)

Lesson: He addressed the problem

When the Samaritans refused to welcome Jesus in their cities, the Disciples proposed:

"Lord, do You want us to command fire to come down from heaven and consume them, just as Elijah did?"

Instead of:

"I cannot believe how wicked you are!"

Jesus' rebuke was:

"You do not know what manner of spirit you are of. For the Son of Man did not come to destroy men's lives but to save them." (Luke 9:55-56-NKJV)

Lesson: He addressed the evil spirit and invoked the righteous spirit, correcting the problem!

When, after His resurrection, the disciples told Thomas:

"We have seen the Lord!"

Thomas answered:

"Unless I see the nail marks in his hands and put my finger where the nails were, and put my hand into his side, I will not believe."

Jesus appeared a week later to all of them and said to Thomas:

"Put your finger here; see my hands. Reach out your hand and put it into my side."

He attacked the problem directly! And since Thomas had declared: *"I will not believe"*, Jesus added: *"Do not be faithless and incredulous, but [stop your unbelief and] believe! "(Jn20:25-27-Amplified Bible)*. In other words: *"Stop proclaiming unbelief on yourself, and do the opposite!"*
Lesson: not only The Lord addressed the problem, but He also led Thomas to annul a bad proclamation on himself and to start doing the right thing!

Last but not least, after His resurrection, when confronting Peter while he and all the remaining disciples had backslidden into being fishermen,

Jesus did not say: *"Peter, you are a backslider!"*

Rather: *The third time He (Jesus) said to him,*

"Simon son of John, do you love me?" Peter was hurt because Jesus asked him the third time, "Do you love me?" He said, "Lord, you know all things; you know that I love you." Jesus said, "Feed my sheep" (Jn20:17).

In other words: *Peter, remember your love for me?... still good? Ok, fine! That's all I want to know; let's not even mention the past, I restore you! Done!*

Lesson: the heavenly model for Bridegroom-Bride is telling us that in some situations where things are so badly compromised, you may simply need to restore each other without any other process, as long as your love for each other is intact!

So, whenever confronting individual issues with His disciples, Jesus always addressed either the problem or the spirit behind, or both! He never attacked the person!

That is our Master's blueprint: when facing an issue with a family member, you should always use your words to attack the problem or the spirit behind; sometimes just restore him/her in the name of love, but never, ever attack the person!

A few samples from our Participants, of how to address issues:

1-"Honey, we have to find a solution to this issue of procrastination"

Instead of : *"you are so, so lazy!"*

2-"Sweetheart, let's pray to cast away the enemy's attack on our finances"

Instead of: *"You keep squandering our entire family budget on useless things!"*

3-"Darling, do you still love me?"

Instead of *"you are disrespectful, mean and rude to me!"*

4-Let's pray to protect your relation with Mom and Dad!
Instead of *"you're such a selfish, spoiled brat!"*

5- "May God open your intelligence and grant you wisdom!"
instead of *"you are a no-good, dumb and stupid child!"*

6-"This kind of behavior is unacceptable" versus *"you are the shame of this family!"*

7-"spirit of poverty, I cast you out of my family!"
instead of *: "My husband/wife (or my family) is always broke, we're so poor!" etc...*

Finally, when Peter betrayed Him according to the exact words that the Lord had given earlier to the disciples (moreover, Peter had declared: "*Even if I have to die with you, I will never disown you." - Matt 26: 31-35.*), instead of: "*Hey Peter, see how presumptuous you are?"*

The Lord's reaction was a simple look straight in Peter's eyes.
Result?

And he (Peter) went outside and wept bitterly.
(Luke 22:61-62)

Lesson: sometimes, when the fault, the harm incurred, and the guilt are blatantly obvious, no need to say anything!

A simple eye-to-eye confrontation without a word can produce deep repentance beyond any proclamation!

Conclusion: In every situation, please pray that the Lord give you the right way to address the problem, or to attack the spirit behind, without ever attacking your beloved ones through your proclamation!

May God bless your efforts!

YES TO LAW N°2 :
The Law of Creation (Part B): SEPARATION

SEPARATION IS A MUST!!

Going back to Genesis 1, verses 1-27, throughout the process of Creation:

First God separated light from darkness, then the water above from the water under the expanse.

He next separated the dry land from the waters; and so on; creating animals was a separation of earth from earth: He took earth from the earth in order to create them.

The Bible says that even for the creation of man, God took dust from the ground; therefore, separating earth from the earth to create man. When creating woman, He separated one rib from the man and created woman.

In other words, the whole creation process was a series of separations.

After the creation of marriage, in Gen2:24, the Bible says:

"For this reason, a man will leave (separate from) his father and mother and be united to his wife. And they will become one flesh".

Marriage, as a matter of fact, is conceived to begin with a separation from father and mother.

This separation is not only physical, it is spiritual as well. It is also a matter of fact that the new birth begins by a separation, as Jesus says in Luke 14:26:

Those who come to me cannot be my disciples unless they love me more than they love father and mother, wife and children, brothers and sisters, and themselves as well. (Good News Translation)

Going back to the separation within a marriage, we want to stress, dear reader, how important that matter is to the Lord:

"For this reason, a man will leave (separate from) his father and mother and be united to his wife. And they will become one flesh".

This rule was set in the perfection of God's creation! Before the fall of Man!! In other words, the Lord, in His prescience, had already foreseen that the lack of separation could only spell trouble within a marriage, even in the perfect world of the Garden of Eden!! Please, think about it!

Having dealt with many couples throughout the world, whenever we ask:

"What are the main reasons why couples have problems?"

Consistently they point out the main sources of marriage problems to be:

Self; family; friends; "exes" (past romance partners), external influence.

This speaks of lack of separation.

The question is: "Are you separated?"

HOW DO YOU KNOW THAT YOU ARE SEPARATED IN YOUR MARRIAGE?

The general rule is that anybody—and we mean anybody—who comes into your family, into your house between you and your spouse and becomes a problem, must leave, except for the following circumstances:

-The person wants to correct your sin
-Your children
-Some cases of children from outside relationships

If any other person comes into your family and becomes a problem, you have no choice: That person must go. Now, "how" the person must go is a different problem altogether, but the principle remains: "That person must go."

The reason is simple enough: Since God's plan requires you to separate from your father and your mother in order to be with your spouse, then who else under the sun would be exempt? Your friends? Your exes? Whoever was before?

In the Lord's eyes, marriage is a promotion from Him in order that you have the opportunity to build your own family and legacy with your spouse (Prov 18:22). You need to be separated, that you both may bring about a new family, a new entity, with new standards and values unique to you both, as there is only one such combination worldwide, in time and eternity, with new sets of friends.

It could be former friends and relationships as long they come into your family to be solutions and not problems, to be assets, not liabilities to your healthy relationship.

EXCEPTIONS

Let us go back to the three exceptions to separation stated above:

Exception 1: The person wants to correct your sin.

We remember this young brother in the Lord who was a member of one of our assemblies. He was mistreating his wife and, being a young believer, was still struggling with integrity in financial matters. First the Pastor, then a group of believers went to him and broke it down to him, all in love.

However, his reaction was: "I am no longer feeling comfortable in your midst, so I and my wife must leave this Church."

Obviously he was totally wrong, because the assembly members were actually trying to save him from disaster, which he eventually learned the hard way after leaving.

In this case, shutting out the brethren was not separation unto God; the same could apply to a father, mother, or any other relative or friend, coming to attempt to warn you about a sin, a situation or a behavior that might ultimately bring disaster in your family.

When such a situation occurs, you cannot claim the principle of separation in order to justify your straying away into the path of destruction; these people are usually God's messengers to save you and/or your marriage.

Exception 2: Children, particularly those living with you.

This is a no-brainer: by all social laws, and all biblical standards, it is your responsibility to raise and correct your children. (Prov 22:6, Eph 6:4)

Exception 3: The delicate case of children from outside relationships

In Genesis 16, Sarah single-handedly organized that her servant Hagar sleep with Abraham; Hagar conceived a baby: Ishmael. Afterwards, when Sarah had her own son Isaac, she asked her husband to get rid of the young boy (Gen 21: 10).

Obviously the young boy had become a problem: Ishmael was mocking her, disrespecting her, and thereby undermining her honor and her authority, and so she decided that he must go.

Many men in Abraham's shoes would have brought the matter to the Lord probably thinking: "Why would she ask me to get rid of my own son? Hey, she is the one who did this, she is the one who brought this whole matter to existence, she is the one who is responsible for his birth and all, therefore I'm sure God will tell her that she cannot separate me from my dear son Ishmael."

However, in verse 12, God told Abraham that Sara was right, and the boy had to go!

We have seen a lot of couples destroyed by children born of relationships before or after marriage; those kids born out of wedlock are sometimes brought into the family. More often than not, their presence is destructive and—because of lack of separation—one or both spouses allow the whole family to be destroyed by their bad influence.

In the case of Abraham, amazingly, God settled the matter:

"The boy must go".

Why?

Prayerfully asking for answers on this topic, we received the following:

Peace is the key!

From Old to New Testament, peace—particularly in the home—is arguably a crucial element for any real blessing, or any true fulfillment! As the Lord said in Mark 3:25,

And if a house is divided against itself,
that house cannot stand.

There can be no real success or victory where there is strife, division or lack of peace (Gal 5 :15). As a matter of fact, the Lord guarantees that a divided house will be defeated in its daily struggles, battles, and projects.

Question: Why is that? Answer: Unanswered prayers!

When there is strife, permanent disagreements within a home, it translates into the annulment of this sure promise from the Lord:

"Again I say to you that if two of you agree on earth concerning anything that they ask, it will be done for them by My Father in heaven. (Matt 18:19)

The only condition for Victory is agreement!

Therefore, in these situations of "open wars" caused by children from outside relationships, very often, it all boils down to a simple question:

"Do we sink together, staying together by all means, or do we give each party a real chance to prosper separately?"

Otherwise said, which of the following is the lesser evil:

"Together, defeat is guaranteed"

versus

"Separated, not ideal, but at least
each of us has a real chance to succeed"?

Therefore, this is the rationale behind the next part.

Please, do not misunderstand us: Every situation is different, so you have to be very careful to discern how to behave in your specific case.

Note this: as long as people get along and there is no major and insurmountable problem of incompatibility, please go to the next step: this does not apply to your case.

Therefore we will only consider circumstances where:

- You and your spouse have diligently exhausted all spiritual avenues (prayer, fasting, etc…) to no avail.
- There is a blatant incompatibility between that child of yours and your present spouse/children; and

-all humanly possible steps and mediation for a peaceful resolution of issues have been exhausted, to no avail; and

-physical separation appears to be the lesser evil, as all parties are just plain miserable under present conditions.

Case 1: The child is from a previous marriage and lives with you.

You cannot send the child away in the event of problems, as it is assumed that you and your new wife/husband agreed upon raising that child prior to your wedding. Therefore, it is considered to be just another problem with one of your natural children, and it is the responsibility of both of you to solve the issue.

However, if the former spouse, that is, the "ex", also has some custody of the child and is the one instigating the child's misbehavior, it may be best to give up custody of the child while taking steps for continuing to provide for all that child's needs.

Case 2: The child is from a previous marriage and does not live with you.

In this case it is best to take steps, in perfect accord with your spouse, to pay your support and conduct your visitation outside the privacy of your home, thus avoiding uneasy contact between the two clashing entities as much as possible.

Case 3: The child is born out of wedlock before you met your present wife/husband, and has been legally entrusted to your custody.

Just as in the first case, it is your child; you have the responsibility to raise him.

However, if your "ex" is trying to win back custody and is the main cause of your troubles with the child, as we said before, separation here would mean to consider the possibility of giving up custody of the child, while fulfilling your legal duties from afar.

Case 4: The child is born out of wedlock before you met your present wife/husband, and lives with you outside legal custody.

Again, the matter should have been settled before your present marriage; the same as Case 1 and Case 3: it is your duty to raise the child!

Case 5: The child is born out of wedlock after you met your present wife/husband, and you have legal custody.

This is a case of infidelity: The wedding bed has been soiled and the fruit of it (the child) will almost always bite you and your family—it's just a matter of time.

If your marriage survived that tsunami, be thankful to God for your spouse and/or legitimate children, but please don't push it to the point of imposing the presence of that bitter fruit of infidelity in your home. It would be like sticking it down their throats! By far the lesser harm would be to take all the peaceful steps and entrust the child to the other parent.

Case 6: The child is born out of wedlock after you met your present wife/husband, and you have no custody.

Again, it is a case of infidelity that usually leads to tragic clashes and reminders in your marriage.

You should not even consider claiming custody and should remove the child as far as possible from your household setting, while paying your social dues for its provision.

LACK OF SEPARATION: THE VIRUS

The lack of separation is the single most lethal virus for healthy marriages.

FIVE MAIN SOURCES OF LACK OF SEPARATION: THE "FEARSOME FIVESOME"

The Virus of Lack of Separation in marriages, most of the times, comes from the following, that we call the "Fearsome Fivesome":

-Self
-Family
-Friends
-Exes and their children
-Some cases of bad counselors

SELF or EGO

"The two shall become one" means implicitly that the first separation when taking the decision to enter a marriage should be the separation:

From "me" to "us-as-one"!
From "I" to "we-as-one"!

Amazingly, in spite of all the pre-marital preparation and counseling, most problems in a marriage are rooted in the difficulty, failure or refusal to pro-actively undergo that separation, particularly in the beginning stages of the process; unfortunately, the scars left by those early skirmishes due to egos can be irreparable and prove lethal in the long run.

Actually, in every decision, plan, behavior (or even attitude), as well as any action, wish, engagement, or relationship (old and new), the lack of separation from "me" unto "we-are-now-one" indeed is the root of all the other separation problems.

FAMILY

From the dawn of time, it has always been a natural, normal human behavior to cling to the ones we love and to refuse to let go of them, particularly in the case of parents-children relationships, where so much has been invested for so long in Time, Love, Material and Finances, Dreams and Expectations.

Therefore, is it really a surprise that separation become a major issue in case the beloved child goes to marriage? Again, God, in His divine wisdom, foresaw this; even before the fall of Man, even before the first sin, while He was still marveling at the perfection of His creation, the Lord declared:

Therefore a man shall leave his father and mother and be joined to his wife, and they shall become one flesh.
(gen 2:24)

In fact, sometimes those issues in marriages occur because:

Some family members refuse the separation;

One or both spouses also refuse to own up to their new status and continue to cling to their respective family members, to the detriment of their marriage;

A mix of all the above.

FRIENDS (OLD AND NEW)

Old Friends

The same things which we said for families apply to friends, to some extent. Usually, the longer the friendship (for example from childhood), the more they behave like family members.

Problems can occur when one or both parties want to continue "as before your spouse came into the mix", particularly when those friendly old (and sometimes new) habits are conflicting with your marriage agenda.

New Friends

Issues of separation can occur, not always from old friends, but also from new friendships made after you met your spouse or after your marriage.

Getting to know each other deeper usually exposes their weaknesses and sometimes behavioral clashes with your new friends that can quickly destroy the unity of a marriage if separation is not immediately addressed.

In fact, we always strongly recommend in our marriage counseling sessions that deep and strong new friendships and relations be dealt with the other way around:

A couple should carefully study the character of new friends before having a deeper relationship with them, mostly on the biblical criteria stated in

Do not be so deceived and misled!
Evil companionships (communion, associations) corrupt and deprave good manners and morals and character.
(1 Cor 15:33 Amplified Bible)

We presume that it is clearly understood that companions with sinful habits should be avoided, except for cases where you are in the active process of witnessing to them with the clear goal of winning them to the Lord. If that's the case, a line should be drawn in order for you to never participate in their sin.

That being said, based on the usual experience from our seminars, special attention should be paid to the following categories of new friends:

Bitter and negative people
Idle and single persons
New people from the opposite sex

The bitter and negative or everly pessimistic people usually sow their attitude into your marriage for almost any situation. Sooner or later you will find yourself looking at your marital issues according to some degree of their world view.

The idle and single just don't have the same issues or agendas as you and your spouse, and many a married couple have been destroyed by the influence of such a person.

The red flag of all, is building new friendships with the opposite sex. We will discuss that later in this chapter.

"EXES" AND THEIR PROGENIES

Ex-girlfriends/boyfriends and ex-husbands/wives can easily turn to be the ultimate marriage killers. It is never a good thing to have them mixed at any level with your marriage because, some way, somehow, they always bring along their truckload of:

Anger and/or jealousy
Bitterness
Reminders of the past
Comparisons with your spouse
Blaming you for past failures
Crediting him/her for past successes
Using children with you as a visa into your privacy to make your marriage miserable.

Most of all, there's a love/hate or hate/love relationship that is always a direct threat to your marriage ("It's a thin line between love and hate," says the song), not only because of what you do, but also of what you don't do.

Your spouse is always on high alert when you are around your ex and might misinterpret or get the wrong signal from any action or inaction, deed or omission, spoken or unspoken word, body language, facial expression, noise or even silence.

THE RARE CASE OF BAD COUNSELORS

This is by far the least category in terms of the rate of occurrence, yet one of the most dangerous in case of deviation, for one good reason: Most often, at least one of the spouses totally trusts the counselor; therefore when there is a separation issue, it can become a long uphill battle, leaving many long-term scars in the couple.

Again, the problem can go two ways: Sometimes it is one or both spouses who cannot separate themselves from their spiritual leader or counselor, and sometimes it is the pastor, elder, marriage counselor etc…, who steps into a marriage beyond his/her boundaries for a broad range of reasons: False doctrine, power abuse, over-controlling spirit, financial/material exploitation or other gain, personal spiritual or other agenda.

The nuisance capacity of this category and the feuds and all kind of problems that they can generate between husband and wife could be devastating and lethal to entire families and marriages.

THE RED FLAG: if, for any reason at all, you consider the spiritual counselor to be more worthy of respect and honor than your own spouse, then something is totally wrong!

FIVE BATTLEGROUNDS FOR SEPARATION

There are five major resources which represent the battlegrounds for separation in every marriage:

Unto the Lord
Emotions
Quality time
Finances/material resources
Home privacy

Battleground No 1:
Separation unto The Lord

In fact this is the greatest separation that covers them all. It is that separation to establish the Lord as the supreme authority in your marriage, therefore to serve and honor Him through your good testimony, and particularly, to obey His Word.

Luke 14:26-Contemporary English Version (CEV):
You cannot be my disciple, unless you love me
more than you love your father and mother,
your wife and children, and your brothers
and sisters. You cannot come with me
unless you love me more than
you love your own life.

Separation unto the Lord means having the mindset you will always choose God's ways and prescription in any issue; that you will never commit a sin in order to please anyone, including your father and mother, your wife and children, your brothers and sisters, or even yourself.

Separation Battleground No 2: Emotions

Actually, Separation is for our own good!!

Take our emotions for example:

It's so easy to love the good. How about when the good disappears? This is where the Lord steps in. The Bible says in Rom 5:8:

But God demonstrates His own love toward us, in that while we were still sinners, Christ died for us.

We carnally love BECAUSE. Welcome to the love DESPITE! The heavenly model of love between the bridegroom and the bride is the love DESPITE. Welcome to the true love!

Returning to the heavenly model of Christ the bridegroom and the Church, His bride in Luke 14:26-27:

"You cannot be my disciple, unless you love me more than you love your father and mother, your wife and children, and your brothers and sisters. You cannot come with me unless you love me more than you love your own life." (CEV)

It is as if Jesus is saying: deny your poor "Love Because" for you wife, husband, father, mother, sister, brother, and yourself. In exchange, take the real love, my "love despite" that will make you love them when there is nothing more to be loved in them! Take the unconditional love of God!

This is why it is for our own good to be separated spiritually unto the Lord!

The main categories of people concerned about our emotions are our spouse, children and household, family, Christian family, friends and colleagues, enemies … and the rest of the world.

Looking at the heavenly model of the Christ-Church relationship as the perfect model for marriage by God's standards, the Word says:

From him (Jesus or the Bridegroom) the whole body, joined and held together by every supporting ligament, (Bridegroom and Bride bound together as one) grows and builds itself up in love, as each part does its work. (Eph 4:16)

God's perfect plan is that the body of Christ be the Dispatcher of God's love as we witness to the World!

In the same way, the Husband should pour all his love into his bride so that together, as one, they dispatch love to all around them. This means particularly that any relationship with the opposite sex should, somehow, involve your spouse (an issue we will address later).

OTHER SEPARATION BATTLEGROUNDS: QUALITY TIME, FINANCES/MATERIAL RESOURCES, HOME PRIVACY:

One verse says it all:
"And the two shall become one flesh" (Gen 2:24, Eph 5:31)
Your spouse must have it all!!

In God's eyes, you and your spouse are one, and therefore Separation unto the Lord and his Word is key (trust that God means what his word says for your marriage).

After that, 100% of these four resources, (that is, your Emotions, Quality time, Material possessions and/or finances, Privacy), are meant to be focused first on your marriage (acting as one). Then together as one, you and your spouse should manage how much of each will be shared with those elements external to your marriage:

Spiritual activities, families including adoptions, children from outside relationships, friends and colleagues, and the rest of the world.

The mistake that many make is in trying to distribute those resources on their own, while excluding their spouse, even when the latter holds the great majority of it all. By not acting as one, this opens up the pathway for problems and trouble in a marriage.

The issue is not how much of those resources is shared outside; it is the very idea of not acting 100% as one on these matters:
For example, one little glimpse of emotion outside of your marriage, one minute of quality time with the wrong person, one gift of 10 cents to the wrong person, letting the wrong person inside the privacy of your home for one minute: any of these could spell disaster for your family and your marriage!

HOW TO SEPARATE FROM PEOPLE?

The process of separation (from people) is sometimes very delicate and really should be always led by the Lord, prayerfully.

We always insist on the Golden Rule: You should always protect your spouse from your family, friends and exes, and vice versa! Always place yourself as a shield to protect your spouse; never let her/him be in a position of direct confrontation with people you personally need to be separated from.

In our case for instance, I (Roger) am always the one to address any issue with my own family, thus leaving my Darling (Vicky) totally out of it! I (Vicky) am always the one to address any issue with my own family, thus leaving my Darling (Roger) totally out of it!

HOW DO YOU DEAL WITH THE OPPOSITE SEX?

In the above passage (Eph 4:16), again making the analogy between Christ and his Church (his body, his bride) on one side, then husband and wife on the other side, the scripture insists that the Husband should pour all his love into his bride so that together, as one body, they dispatch love to all around them and particularly in any relationship; this, of course, applies to the sensitive relationships with the opposite sex.

Any relationship with the opposite sex should, somehow, involve your spouse; especially, you should put an end to any relationship with the opposite sex the minute your spouse becomes uncomfortable with it.
Why?

Because the great majority of cases of immorality and infidelity in Christian marriages begin with a careless, "innocent" relationship with the opposite sex. Yet, the Bible is clear:

Flee from sexual immorality. (1 Cor 6:18)

We remember one pastor who, from the pulpit made this point particularly clear with his statement:

"Me and my wife are one, and we do everything together. I never counsel women alone; she must be present. This is not a subject open for debate: in my assembly, you can take it or leave it."

Another time, we attended an international meeting of pastors and great Christian leaders, and at one point this question was raised:

"As a pastor, how do you handle immorality issues?"

After a long, long debate on the subject, there was only one conclusion:

Flee from sexual immorality!

How many scandals have destroyed Christian leaders and Churches through the years, simply because they could not apply this precious, irrevocable biblical warning?
God knows better!!

We have heard many pastors preach:

"If you still are afraid to be alone with a sister, then you are still not mature enough"!

How dangerous!!

There are four dimensions to the problem: Your own emotions, the emotions of the other person, the testimony of the World watching you, and last but not least, the schemes of the enemy!

You can only control **Dimension 1** (or can you?), and assuming as they say that "you are mature enough", you still have no control whatsoever over the other three dimensions.

Dimension 2: The other person's emotions are absolutely beyond your control no matter how many precautions you take to keep a pure and innocent relationship.

Dimension 3: The testimony of the World watching you.

Assuming that Dimension 1 and Dimension 2 are ok and under control, how do you control **Dimension 3**? That is, what is the perception of those watching you, particularly in a world where sexual immorality has become, by far, the No.1 tool in advertising?

We always remember that big sign on the Highway MD 140 between Baltimore and Westminster, Md:

"*Teach your children that VIRGIN is not a dirty word"*

Dimension 4: The enemy's schemes.

It is well documented that many a time the enemy has sent his agents to compromise the integrity and testimony of Christian leaders worldwide, and most of the times, just like in the biblical example of Joseph who was framed by Potiphar's wife, it boils down to "you said… she said"!

Guess who the World believes in 99.99% of those cases?
Conclusion:

Flee from sexual immorality (1 Cor 6:18)

HOW DO YOU FLEE FROM IMMORALITY?

The best answer is to involve your spouse in every relationship you have with the opposite sex! How? Ask for God's wisdom depending on the situation.
Here are some hints from personal experience:

Concerning your "exes"

Proactively tell your spouse about your exes, particularly before marriage if possible; that can be a painful experience, but always a rewarding one.

If any of your exes attempts to contact you for any reason at all, be sure to fully involve your spouse in every bit of the meetings, conversations or other communications, and let the "ex" know that these are your terms; for example, "cc" every email to your spouse.

At work:

Always wear your wedding ring;

Display your spouse's photos;

Always call him/her at your break time, and particularly when alone in a work environment with a colleague of the opposite sex;

Bring him/her up often, in the brightest way possible, in office conversations, particularly when things turn personal;

Never, ever complain about your spouse in your work environment.

Always present your spouse's best side when you do speak of him/her.

In general, when you let it be known how much you value

your marriage and how dearly you love your spouse, that mere fact will protect you from 99% of the attempts and other schemes for immorality.

In Church and social settings:

Only one rule: Always involve your spouse in every relationship.

IN CONCLUSION:

Separation is a must; it is not optional, and the lack of separation is the single most insidious and destructive virus of marriages. In short: have no secrets with your spouse.

The root change

First, you must separate unto God, that's for your most good! Therefore, you must endeavor to obey His prescriptions for your marriage!

Even in the Perfection of the Garden of Eden, God had already prescribed Separation as a must for a Glorious marriage, and this, prior to the fall of Man. Think about it! You and your spouse are one in God's eyes!

When it comes to your emotions, your quality time, your financial and material resources, and your privacy, this oneness translates:

Focus 100% of these resources on your spouse, and together, manage them in one accord, then turn to the Lord and say:

Thank you Lord Jesus, I am separated!

Alleluia!!

CHAPTER I I I

YES TO LAW N°3: THE LAW OF SEEDS

VICKY

"At workshop No.1, the speaker said, we had to list "the 10 most usual problems and issues we face daily in our marriages." So, here goes:

Quarrels.
Bad communication
Selfishness
Family and friends
Finances
Unfaithfulness/disloyalty
Unfulfilled sex life
Lack of respect
Rebellion
Lack of prayer

A burst of applause echoed through the luxurious seminar hall as the speaker made his way back to his seat; yet, it was somehow shy, as if the audience was feeling guilty of being exposed.

My Darling, who was the seminar facilitator, felt the

tension and immediately introduced the lady speaker for workshop No.2.

She stepped forward, again to the sound of applause and declared: "In this workshop, we had to answer the following question: 'What do you expect from your Marriage?". Here are the top 10 answers:

Love
Understanding
Faithfulness
Patience
Love of God
Peace and Harmony
Good sex life
Good communication
Care
Loyalty

The audience broke into applause and showered her with pats on her back, high-fives, and "Bravo's!" as she made her way back to her seat.

At that moment, my darling spoiled the party with a seemingly innocent question:

"By the way, those nice things you expected out of your marriage..., when did you sow them?"

The audience was totally silent, while all looked down.

My darling continued:

"Let me rephrase it: Think about all the things you have actually been sowing into your marriage of late; that's just about the first list. How could they possibly grow and become anything like that second beautiful list you just gave us?"

Again, total silence…

" Brethren, look no more; this is the heart of your problem: Sowing quarrels, selfishness, distrust etc…, yet expecting peace and harmony, understanding etc… really? That's sowing weeds, thorns and thistles and expecting mangoes, apples, oranges and other beautiful fruits."…

SOWING: THE FIRST TASK ASSIGNED TO MAN BY GOD

The first and only job God assigned to Man was sowing (Genesis 2). Looking at the World today, it's obvious that being a farmer is far, far from being the only bread-winning activity!

And yet, if you look carefully, you will see that, in fact, in every productive field of activity, it's all about sowing:

Every child is the result of father and mother sowing not only each other's seed, but also sowing love into each other!

Raising that child is the action of parents sowing their love, life and experience into him or her.

Education is the action of teachers sowing their own knowledge and experience into their students.

Finally, manufacturing is sowing raw products into a system that will yield the desired marketable end-products.

Every business is all about sowing money to make money:

Yes, Life is all about sowing! Do you have a problem? Check the seed!

Of course, Marriage, that great part of life, is all about sowing, too.

How? The Bible says in Galatians 6:7:
"Everyone will reap whatever he has sowed." with "whatever" including the spiritual.

There are so many passages in the Bible showing that everything that you sow is what you will reap, in regards to money, emotions, and feelings! That applies, of course, to Christian life in general, and to marriage in particular.

HOW DOES THE SOWER PROCEED?

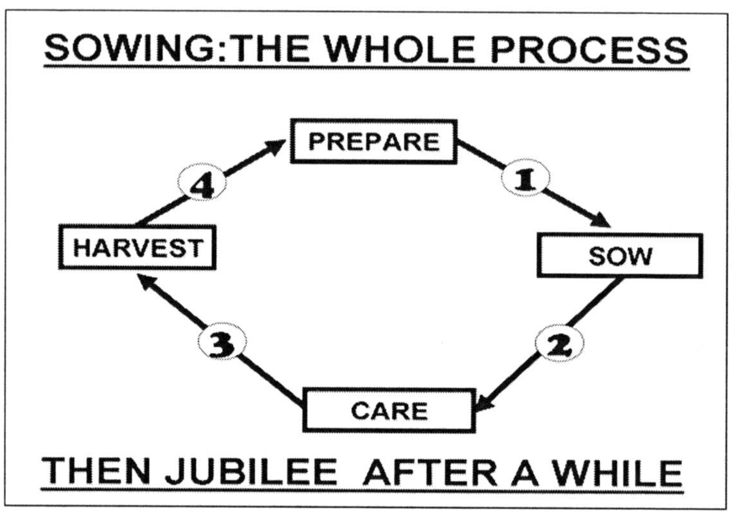

Usually, when you ask anyone who does farming about how to proceed, it goes this way:

-The seed must be determined in advance.

-First you have to clean and make the ground ready: preparation.

-After that, the seeding itself, meaning you plant the seeds in the soil.

-Third, after planting, you must water, take care of the plant, and be patient until it grows to something consumable; call it caring.

-Finally, of course, is the long awaited time of harvest, and then you reap.

WAITING: ARROWS 1, 2, AND 3

In between all those phases, you need time and patience: That's why between the very first step of preparation and the harvest, you have a growing process lasting anywhere from 3 months to years, depending on the type of fruit.

ARROW 4: RE-SET AND START OVER- IT'S A CYCLE!

Question: Once you reap, do you just settle down and say: "Ok, I'm rich forever"? Of course, not. It is a continuing process—a cycle. Usually, it's a yearly cycle that goes with the seasons.

JUBILEE

Moreover, the Bible calls for a certain time when you let the land rest: The Sabbath of the Land biblically occurred every seven years. The Jubilee occurred every 50 years, which called for some kind of a celebration, re-setting and freedom.

APPLICATION TO YOUR MARRIAGE

One powerful scripture in the Bible is the parable of the sower found in Matthew 13:

Then He spoke many things to them in parables, saying: "Behold, a sower went out to sow. And as he sowed, some seed fell by the wayside; and the birds came and devoured them. Some fell on stony places, where they did not have much earth; and they immediately sprang up because they had no depth of earth. But when the sun was up they were scorched, and because they had no root they withered away. And some fell among thorns, and the thorns sprang up and choked them. But others fell on good ground and yielded a crop: some a hundredfold, some sixty, some thirty.

and continuing in verses 18-19:

"Therefore hear the parable of the sower: When anyone hears the word of the kingdom, and does not understand it, then the wicked one comes and snatches away what was sown in his heart

WHAT SEED?

The Word tells us that the field is the heart. There are many passages in the Bible describing the fruit, and all refer either to an actual physical fruit, or to some type of fruit of character. The best illustration is found in Galatians 5:

But the fruit of the Spirit is love, joy, peace, longsuffering, kindness, goodness, faithfulness, gentleness, self-control.

When we hold our marriage seminars, usually the first question that we ask is:
"What do I expect from marriage?"
Most people list all those wonderful things they were expecting out of marriage.

The second question we ask usually is:
"What are the most common problems facing marriages?"
Again, the participants list a series of painful things they usually go through, day in and day out. Most of the time, going through individual counselling, for the majority of them, they are simply stating:

"The answers to question 1 are where we are aspiring to get; yet, on a daily basis, what we are actually sowing into our marriages and spouses are those things listed as answers to question 2."

To which we always make this point:
"Ok, this is the fruit that you're expecting from your marriage, this is what you were expecting from your spouse. Question: -and we want you please to stop and read once again your answer and think for a while-
"When did you sow? Have you applied the seeding procedures?"

What we are saying is that the same sowing process, according to the Word of the Lord, should be applied to marriage: You will only reap whatever you have been sowing.

To further illustrate this, a correlation can be made between the physical planting and sowing process and the one in the spiritual. Allow us to draw your attention to another aspect of the sowing process.

APPLYING TO YOUR MARRIAGE

We usually ask in our seminars:
"What kind of problems can the sower encounter at the stage 1 of the above Sowing Process diagram?"

The usual answers include rocks, infertility, thistles, bad weather, bites, dirt, mud, dust, and in Africa most of the time you will even meet snakes, scorpions and some other dangerous animals, etc.

In both the spiritual sense and in marriage, rocks, infertility, thistles, bad weather, bites, mud, and dust all stand for problems like moods, physical problems, character issues, confrontations, and so on.

Of course snakes stand for the devil. You will encounter all kinds of tricks from the enemy, whose No.1 goal is to destroy Christian marriages.

Question: Have you ever seen a serious farmer complain and loose his joy or give up, just because he met some sort of obstacle while he was doing his job?
The answer is usually “No”.
Why? Because he keeps his eyes on the prize, which is the harvest. So he keeps his joy and nothing will take it away.

The problems encountered during the preparation process are more or less the same as those encountered during the seeding process; more or less the same as those during the caring process; but again, the eyes of the sower remain fixed on the harvest. So he keeps his joy.

Finally, the blessed time of the harvest arrives. The sower usually doesn’t even remember those problems encountered because of the joy of the harvest.

One thing that we have learned in our marriage is that the same applies.

The Lord started revealing those things to us sometime during the mid 90’s when He made us confront the disparity between what each of us was hoping to get from our marriage versus what each of us was actually sowing into it!

We realized that we had been lying to ourselves! We came to face the hard truth that the list of the things we both had been sowing into our marriage was composed by a great majority of the very negative things each of us was grumbling and complaining about every day!

From then on, things changed, and the good seeding process started. And from experience, we can guarantee you that victory is at hand as long as a couple is ready to go through the sowing process as follows:

First, in advance, make a list of what you expect out of your marriage and/or spouse.

Then, for each item (seed), one at a time:

Prepare the ground: Each person is different. You might, for instance, prayerfully find the right way, the right time, the right setting, the right place, or the right occasion to sow! Be prepared to encounter all kinds of character and other issues; yet, you must gladly keep up!

Sow: Again this will depend on each personality. We highly recommend Gary Chapman's excellent book "The Five Love Languages" as a very useful tool to help you choose the best way to plant that love seed into your beloved spouse, according to his/her own distinct "love language."

Care: Time to be patient, to pray while keeping on doing the right things, and keeping your joy and peace while resting assured that the Lord is making the seed grow in the unseen until it appears in plain sight.

Remember, first appear the flowers, but as beautiful as they may be, they must never be considered to be fruits. For example, your spouse may suddenly make a jaw-dropping move as a first positive response; it is a very promising sign, but consider it to be just a flower!

The difference between the flower and the fruit is that the flower shines with the sunlight, only to wilt or close-up at night-time; whereas, the fruit is more constant under any weather.

The watering and caring process must continue until the flower turns to a real fruit, and still, you have to give it time to ripen! In other words, patience, patience, patience!

Harvest time: Then you will reap!
Actually, many couples around the world apply this process! And, it really works for them... only for a period of time! Why?

MARRIAGE DEADLY VIRUS Nº.2: STOPPING THE SOWING PROCESS AFTER THE FIRST FRUITS, or TAKING YOUR SPOUSE FOR GRANTED

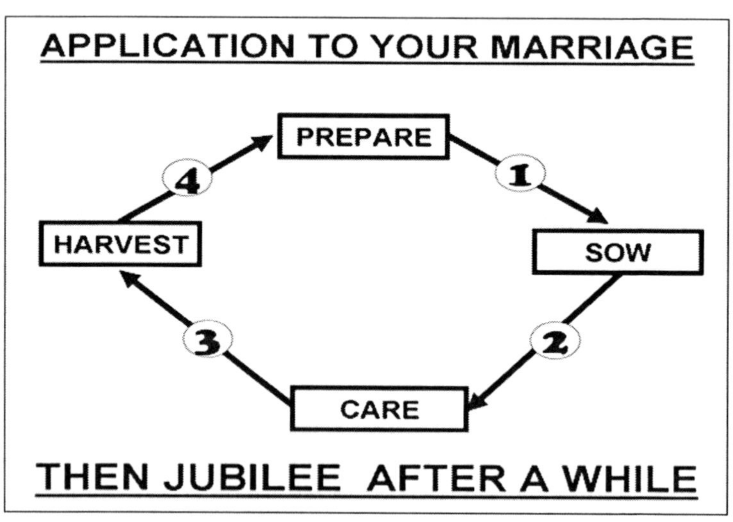

When looking at our Sowing Process diagram again, arrow 4 between the harvest and and back to the preparation phase is a place where many marriages fail. That arrow represents taking the other for granted.

Many couples start off very well, as they go through all this sowing-reaping process. They really endeavour to prepare, to seed, all those nice things. They care and are patient enough until they reap. And that's it! Then they retire! They believe they have it all figured out, then at least one of the spouses begins to take the other for granted and stops all the good things that kept the good love fire burning.

In our seminars, we have been asking:

"What does that mean, to take the other one for granted?"

Here are some of the answers.
Within this sampling, you may see one that applies to your own situation:

- -Lack of respect
- -Neglecting your body and appearance
- -Neglecting your intimacy, etc.
- -Not doing the first things that won your spouse's heart:

    Encouragements, compliments, love letters, speaking with respect and love, meekness and smiling at each other, kindness, sweetness and gentleness, reminding him/her the privilege to be her/his spouse, holding hands, opening the door for her, honouring him/her, love gestures, love gifts, jokes, etc…
- -Saying the "no-no" of all: "I regret I married you", when you are angry!!

Just as no farmer retires after one or two years of good farming, but instead makes it a life-time endeavour, a great marriage is a lifetime of practicing the seeding process, of keeping the good things that brought each of you to say about the other:

"Thank you Lord, you have given me the perfect one
I want to spend the rest of my life with!"

JUBILEE

Then there's the idea of the Sabbath/Jubilee. After a period of time, it is good to let it rest for a while; to escape from the routine in order to get a fresh start, a renewing boost to your relationship. Some of the recommendations that we have received and seen in our seminars are:

Getting out of the same old routine

Going on vacation together: putting everything else on hold, getting someone to watch the children, so just the two of you can go out!

Taking some time apart—healthy times. For instance, one or the other might visit their parents or family away for a week or two.

Some kind of marital retreat/renewing your vows.

Experience has proved that this is a wonderful refresher for any marriage.

In short, this whole seeding process should be applied consistently.

Dear reader, you will experience your own victory, and in doing so, achieve your own form of Sabbath/Jubilee which is best suited for your marriage.

A perfect illustration of the law of seeds for a marriage is the great movie "Fireproof" from Alex Kendrick, who co-wrote and co-produced it with Stephen Kendrick. We highly recommend it for all Christian marriages.

Long story short (without spoiling the suspense if you have not yet seen it), the whole movie can be summed up in one sentence: Caleb was given by his dad a list of positive things to sow into his marriage and his spouse, according to all the principles of farming, which he did, with the end result of saving his marriage!

FINALLY WHAT IS CHRISTIAN LIFE?

What was Christian life meant to be from the standpoint of marriage?

Step 1: In the Spirit and in Truth from Your Own Heart

The starting point is in your heart. Christian life was meant to be a life of worshipping the True God from one's deepest heart in the Spirit and in Truth (John 4:23-24); the fruit that you desire to reap is Love, Joy, Peace, Patience, Kindness, Goodness, Faithfulness, Gentleness, Self-control (Galatians 5:22-23).

Step 2: Sowing Into Your Spouse

For husbands, the Bible says:

Husbands, love your wives (Ephesians 5:25)

Then:

Love suffers long and is kind; love does not envy; love does not parade itself, is not puffed up; does not behave rudely, does not seek its own, is not provoked, thinks no evil; does not rejoice in iniquity, but rejoices in the truth; bears all things, believes all things, hopes all things, endures all things. Love never fails (1 Cor13:4-8).

For wives:

Wives, likewise, be submissive to your own husbands, that even if some do not obey the word, they, without a word, may be won by the conduct of their wives, when they observe your chaste conduct accompanied by fear (1 Pet 3:1).

A man should sow love into his wife, while a wife should sow respect and good character into her spouse, to the point that even an unbelieving husband may be won by the gospel without a word!

Step 3: Sowing Into Your Household and Family

From there, the Bible says:

"*If anyone does not know how to manage his own family, how can he take care of God's Church? (1 Timothy 3:5*)

Therefore, as a Christian, my next duty is to sow into my household and to make sure to have victory there.

Step 4: Sowing Into the World

The next step is the Lord's calling for us:

Go therefore and make disciples of all the nations... (Matt 28:19)

"The Great Commission" was further explained just before the Lord ascended into Heaven when He said:

"You will be my witnesses." (Acts 1:8)

The Lord calls us principally to preach the Gospel by our witnessing. Therefore, people must be witnesses of what our life is.

So after winning over my home, the next step is winning over everybody observing me, starting with my unbelieving family, my unbelieving colleagues at work, my neighbors, and everybody who's involved in some way with me: my banker, lawyer, doctor, Church members, co-workers, family members, and so on.

THE "CHURCH": A SPIRITUAL GAS STATION

So, what is the role of what we usually call the "traditional Church" in this whole thing? Many answers are possible, and in our seminars, we've heard many of them. May we suggest the best answer we ever received?

"The Church as we see it today—meetings, prayer, worshipping and so on—is the spiritual gas station where we get all the strength, care, and everything that we need to carry out those Christian duties".

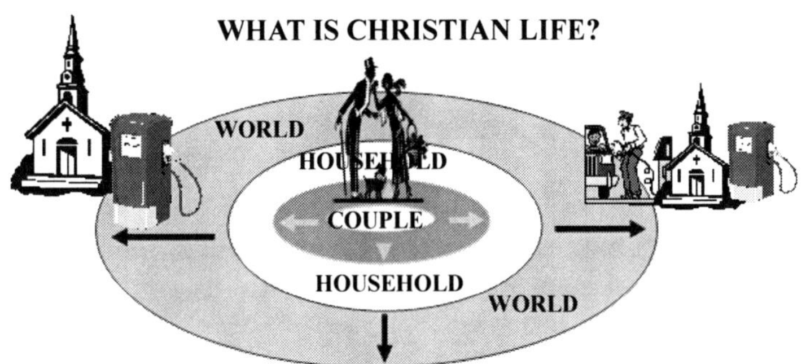

SOWING: THE FIELD OF THE HEART, BEGINNING WITH MY OWN (JN 4-23-24)

Traditionally, a good gas station has everything you need to keep your car running: Gas, oil, fluids, spark plugs, and other quick-fix emergency parts, and sometimes even a repair shop.

In Luke 16, the Bible says that the Good Samaritan (the Lord), after taking care of this wounded man (representing a young convert) entrusted him to an inn, or a hotel.

The Church is that hotel where you have all the care, all the teaching, all the healing, wound patching, deliverance etc., and resting place where you can renew your strength, get everything you need, and then continue.

Nowadays that example of the Church being the gas station sounds to us like an excellent illustration in our modern life of the equivalent of that parable.

Unfortunately, this is where many problems occur. Many believers are convinced that their Christian life is mainly what they do in the building they call Church!

In other words, based on the above illustration, it is like taking a trip from Baltimore to New York City and yet, spending the whole five hours of the trip burning your gas, then refuelling, and on, and on…. while never leaving the first gas station five miles right out of Baltimore! And then, doing the very same thing the next day!

Many believers spend their entire Christian life at the gas station (Church): Increasing their studying and meditating on the Word of God; in short, doing all those wondrous things but not making sure they have a genuine familial and social testimony to offer the World (Acts 1:8).

Please, let there be no misunderstanding: The "Church" as we call it, is very, very important!! Simply put, no car can run without gas, so we all need that spiritual gas to even consider any spiritual trip!

What we are saying is that the gas stop is a very important part of the trip, all right, but just a tiny portion of it! By no means should the fact of stopping at the gas station be considered to be the trip!

TALKING ABOUT SPIRITUAL GAS

In short, all the usual activities recommended by pastors in the Church are seeds which bring the favor (therefore the victory) of the Most High into your life in general and your marriage in particular:

Worshipping in Spirit and in truth,
Reading (listening to) and/or studying the Word, the spiritual seed (Matt13:20)
Reading Christian literature
Brotherly Communion: the place of blessing (Ps 133:1-3)
Individual prayer
Group prayer

Fasting
Giving to God's kingdom
Etc...

Moreover, the Lord said in Matthew 6:33

But seek first the kingdom of God and His righteousness, and all these things shall be added to you.

In other words: sow into the expansion of God's kingdom, sow righteousness and all material blessings will automatically follow you!

Without excluding any of those usual spirituals recommended in most Churches, we want to focus on three special spiritual activities:

READING/LISTENING/STUDYING/ MEMORIZING THE WORD OF GOD

In the beginning was the Word (John 1:1)

and,

I have written to you, young men, because you are strong, and the word of God abides in you, And you have overcome the wicked one. (1 John 2:14)

The Word must have the Premier place in your spiritual life. The more you sow the Word of God into yourself, the stronger Christian you will be; therefore please make sure that your personal spiritual life, as well as your family devotional life are soaked into the Scriptures. Sow the Word in yourself! Sow the Word in your household!

PRAYER – AGAIN

It is the seed par excellence that reaps victory.

"If you believe, you will receive whatever you ask for in prayer." (Matt 21:22)

You can never pray too much for protection and success for your marriage, spouse, children, job, spiritual life, testimony and relationships, good reputation, etc. Please, sow.... in prayer!

Pray without ceasing (1 Thess 5:17)

GIVING TO GOD

In Malachi 3:8-10, The Scripture insists that giving your tithe and offering to God is not optional; it is a must—for your own blessing!

To put it simply, it is like a coin: On one side, a curse—that is if you choose not to give. On the other, miraculous blessings—should you choose obedience.

Indeed, the whole process is explained in 2 Corinthians 9 from verse 6:

[Remember] this: he who sows sparingly and grudgingly will also reap sparingly and grudgingly, and he who sows generously [that blessings may come to someone] will also reap generously and with blessings...
And [God] Who provides seed for the sower and bread for eating will also provide and multiply your [resources for] sowing and increase the fruits of your righteousness [which manifests itself in active goodness, kindness, and charity]. Thus you will be enriched in all things and in every way, so that you can be generous, and [your generosity as it is] administered by us will bring forth thanksgiving to God (Amplified version).

Actually, in the spiritual realm, your life and family life are like a field. Whenever you give your tithe and offering, in reality you are merely (and logically) planting the seed of financial, material and spiritual blessing into your own field, in order to allow God to do what only God can do: make it grow into more blessings.

Not giving to God is therefore like a farmer who prepares the ground, fertilizes it perfectly (that is your perfect spiritual life), then plants nothing (or not enough, for those giving less that the required tithe or 10%); question: what should he expect at harvest time?
Without turning into the prosperity Gospel, the fact is:
Giving to God is really, really for your own good!

Sow righteousness in the Lord and reap amazing blessings of all kinds in your personal life, in your marriage life, in your household, in your social life, in your spiritual life! Sow spiritual!

Root Change

"Yes to Law No.3" means I accept God's own worldview in terms of Christian life for us;

that is, to start sowing the fruit of the Spirit in myself, continuing with my spouse, next with the ones in our household, then move on to be a witness to the neighbourhood, my colleagues at work, and the whole world;
and this being done while:

Continuously refilling as needed at the Church (the spiritual gas station), with what is absolutely indispensable for our life trip: teaching/study of the word, prayers, communion with the Lord, communion with the Church in general, in Secret and in public places as well;

Continuously sowing righteousness in the spiritual, for untold blessings and favour.

May His grace be with you!

CHAPTER IV

YES TO LAW N°4: THE LAW OF SUBMISSION

God has three branches of authority over you:

Family,
Society,
Church.

GOD'S AUTHORITY BRANCH N°1: FAMILY

In 1 Corinthians 11:3, The Bible says:

"Now I want you to realize that the head of every man is Christ, and the head of the woman is man, and the head of Christ is God."

In Ephesians 6-1:

"Children, obey your parents in the Lord, for this is right. Honor your father and mother -which is the first commandment with a promise- that it may go well with you and that you may enjoy a long life on the earth."

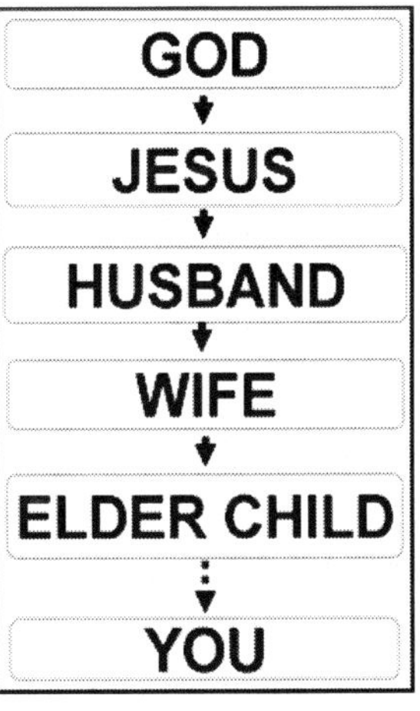

When you put it all together, the Bible is saying that, for each family, God actually functions through a true Power Flow Chart as illustrated at right.

At the top of the chart is God the Father and Jesus immediately after (with the Holy Spirit of course between parentheses).

Immediately thereafter is a branch of power that extends straight to the husband, on to the wife, and then to all the children from the elder child down to you.

That's Power Flow branch No.1.

GOD'S AUTHORITY BRANCH N°2: SOCIETY (NATION, STATE, CITY, EMPLOYER, ETC.)

Secondly, the Bible says in Romans 13:2-4

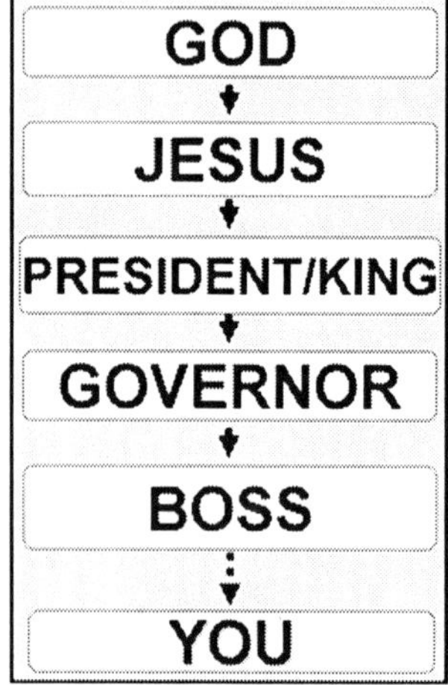

"*there is no authority except that which God has established. The authorities that exist have been established by God. Consequently, he who rebels against the authority is rebelling against what God has instituted, and those who do so will bring judgment on themselves. ...For he is God's servant to do you good. But if you do wrong, be afraid, for he does not bear the sword for nothing. He is God's servant, an agent of wrath to bring punishment on the wrongdoer.*"

The Bible is saying that there is another branch of divine power as seen in the illustration at left, which is obviously independent from the first branch described above.

First God – Jesus – King or President – Governor - whatever their title may be, on down to Mayor and then your Boss, and at the end of the chart, again, it's you.

GOD'S AUTHORITY BRANCH N°3: CHURCH (SPIRITUAL)

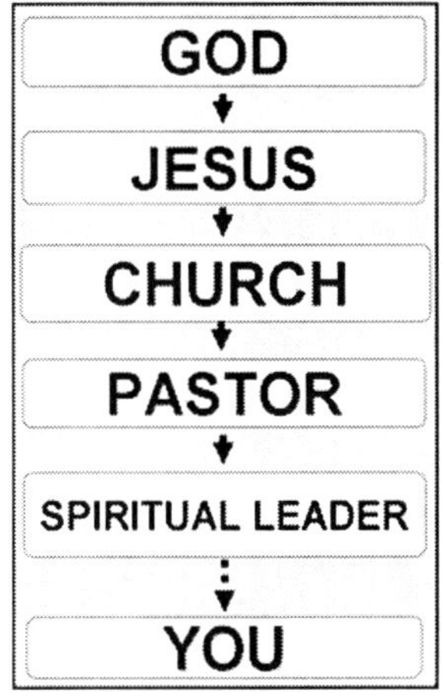

God's third branch of authority is one that, obviously, most of us know very well, which is God – Jesus - the Church - your Pastor – through all the Church organization and spiritual leaders whose authority you are submitted to, and finally you. Again. (Heb 13:17)

All three branches, when put together, look like the diagram below:

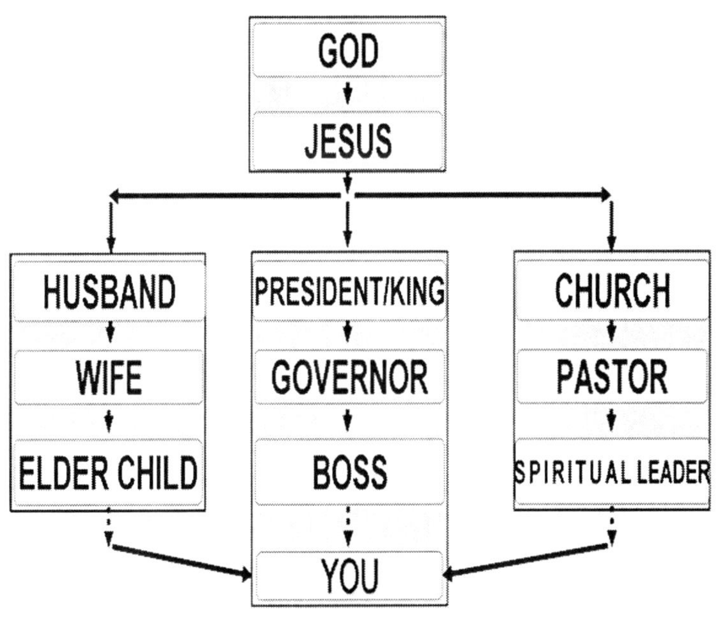

WHY THREE BRANCHES?

Obviously, we are born into families. Obviously, God could have made Adam and Eve and all the many human beings from the creation until today through the same process of taking some dust, blowing into it and creating other humans.

But He sovereignly chose to make us born out of a father and mother in the most precious and important manifestation—the premier action of love.

God was sending a message:
God doesn't want confusion on earth. In a family, there is no doubt where the authority is coming from as it's naturally established.

God clearly said: The husband is at the top, followed by the wife, then by the eldest son, and so on. God first wants you to be born out of love, so that your father and your mother will be the expression and the extension of the hand of love of God for you.

On a daily basis, the role of a governing body is one of protection, security, complementarity, provision, and other crucial social, recreational and emotional activities.

This is what God is doing in His use of the government and the social branch that includes the organization you work for, or where you are studying.

The role of the Church is to unite it all together, with the ultimate Goal of bringing back all humans at the feet of their God and Maker in true worship through Jesus-Christ the Savior, teaching us to know the decrees of God and how to manage our daily life, that we may choose right over wrong in any situation; that is, expanding the Kingdom of God.

Some remarks at this point:

First, the three branches are independent.

Second, similar rules apply inside each branch.

The concept of functional authority applies in all three branches.

In each branch, promotion comes from within, not without!!

True service to God is actually obeying God in all three branches daily.

THE THREE BRANCHES ARE INDEPENDENT

What are we saying?

Take the example of President George W. Bush, 43rd president of the United States, between 2001 and 2009 and whose father served as the 41st president from 1989 to 1993. Now, just imagine that Mr. Bush-the-father comes to visit Bush-the-son during his presidency days and says:

"Son, I don't want X to be your Secretary of department Y; since I am your father, obey me and remove him."

Obviously, it is unthinkable!

Yet, on the other hand, when President Bush-the-son, went into a family meeting, he obviously left his power, his presidential privileges and everything associated with it at the entrance of the house. Whenever he entered that house, the authority shifted to his dad. Within his father's house, his dad could say:

"This is how our family's going to be run."

So the President of the United States, when he goes into his family, is submitted to his parents!

Now, let's continue. When he goes to his Church, is he the one saying, for example:

"Pastor, you know I am the supreme authority of this Nation. Now I order you to appoint my friend X as a new

elder in the Church."?
That would be a national scandal. Guaranteed.

Finally, imagine his Pastor saying:
"Mr. President; when you come here, remember, you are under my authority. As your Pastor, if I don't like somebody in your government, I demand that you just remove him."

How does that sound? Again, the three branches are independent!

INDEPENDENT, YET, THE THREE BRANCHES SHOULD HARMONIOUSLY INTERACT WITH EACH OTHER.

Now, let's get one thing clear:
We're saying that the three are independent, but we're not saying that they should never interact with each other. We're saying that the three should interact, while knowing absolutely where the boundaries are.

Expanding on our previous example, President Bush-the-father should be absolutely welcome to call his son any time of the day or night and say:

"Son, about your government,
I would advise you to do so and so..."

It's just free advice! Any consultation, any advice should absolutely be welcome from the father; and vice versa.
If President Bush-the-son were to attend a family meeting where his dad is the authority, he should be absolutely welcome to say:

"Dad, about such and such issue,
I've tried it another way and this is my advice…"

In the same way, the Pastor of the Church where the President of the USA attends may call him and say:

"Mr President? In the midst of all these
political things, this is what I believe...
I encourage you to do it this way or that way."

Absolutely, the advice is again welcome or vice versa, and, by the way, that is what happens all the time!

The President of the United States may meet the pastor and say:

"Dear Pastor, from my experience as the President of the United States, I would suggest you do so and so... I believe that nominating this person is not very wise..."

In other words, the number one role of the Church as we know it is to be a wise counsel to lead all to the wise pathways of God. All of the branches may interact—not in terms of cross-authority but in terms of counselling; and that is, giving advice to each other, helping each other while knowing that when it comes to the final decision-making, it's up to the authority in that branch.

In general the head of the family doesn't interfere to give orders to his wife or his children within the scope of their social function, just as the social authority (President, Governor, Mayor, Magistrate, etc...) doesn't interfere to give orders to his Church authorities.

As well, the Church should not intervene, to become the authority in the other two branches of God's authority. As a matter of fact, that bad mix was one of the main causes for the French Revolution in 1789 (separation of State from Church), one of the bloodiest civil havocs in recent history.

SIMILAR RULES AND PRINCIPLES INSIDE EACH BRANCH

The three branches have the same functioning rules and principles. For a better understanding, take for example, the social branch:

In 1860, Lincoln was elected President of the United States. The governors of Virginia, Georgia and some other states decided not to submit any longer to his authority as President of the USA. The consequence was the Civil War, the bloodiest war ever in the history of the United States.

In many Churches the same thing has happened. One day, a Pastor—for whatever reason, right or wrong—makes the decision that from now on, he will no longer submit to the authority of another Pastor above him, nor to the whole Church system. This is called "schism" (we've seen quite a few of them), and it is nothing short of a civil war in the hearts of the believers!

We know of one such schism which occurred in an African country. A certain born-again, tongue-speaking denomination wrote to the government against the outgoing group, saying something like: "There is a dangerous sect out there calling themselves "born-again"; please don't allow them to ever meet." What…? One Church calling the government to persecute another Church? Yep!

The same rule applies also in the family:
Anytime the chain of familial authority established by the Creator of marriage is broken at any level, there will be a schism. There will be anarchy; there will be "civil war" in the family.
Welcome to the law of submission: It is a spiritual law!

In the Bible, throughout all the books of Kings and

the Chronicles, that law is continuously at work :

Every time the King was in submission to God and walking with God, the nation was under the blessing.

Every time the governor or the King did not walk with God or did not fear Him, the country was under havoc.

The same thing applies to the other branches of authority.

Now imagine your boss, the head of your office, acting defiantly or openly saying:

"I will not submit to the governing body of our company.
From now on, obey me and only me,
but oppose their orders."

Chances are that office will simply be torn to pieces, exactly a form of civil war!

That's also exactly what happens to every Church where there is a schism and what happens on a daily basis in most families.

Except that most of their members don't realize that the main cause for the majority of family problems is the violation of the law of submission:

When a woman refuses to submit to her husband, there's civil war in the family. When a child decides to not submit to the parents anymore, there's civil war in the family. When the father, the head of the family doesn't have God in his program, or, worse, rebels against God by encouraging a sinful life in his family, you can be sure that what happened to every ungodly king of Israel will happen to his personal kingdom—that is, his family. Disaster is guaranteed.

Again, it's a spiritual law: The main cause of disaster in most families today is the lack of submission to God's chain of authority.

Proof? Let's read the Bible:

CASE 1: YOUNGER BROTHER NOT SUBMITTED TO ELDER BROTHER

Jacob's dealing with his elder brother Esau is the perfect illustration of such consequences; in short:

Jacob fought against his twin brother from the womb, grabbing the heel of Esau on their day of birth (Gen 25:19-25).

When they were young men, Jacob deceived Esau to buy out his eldership (or birthright) for a meal, then later deceived his father, Isaac, and stole Esau's blessing (Gen 27:1-30).

It all generated a deep hatred from Esau, who swore to kill his brother; only God's divine intervention saved Jacob from the wrath of his sibling. Yet, the flame of bad blood kept burning in the following generations:

First, more than 400 years later, Amalek, descendants of Esau, tried to annihilate Israel by attacking them while they were exhausted in the desert after they had left Egypt (Ex 17:8-16).

Then more than 1,000 years later, Haman, a descendant of Agag, the last Amalekite king, planned and almost succeeded in exterminating Israel from the surface of the Earth (Esther 9:23-25).

To the point that God said to Esau's descendents more than 1000 years later:

'Thus says the Lord GOD: "Behold, O Mount Seir (Esau's descendents), I am against you; ... "Because you have had an ancient hatred, and have shed the blood of the children of Israel (Ez 35:3-5).

The Lord Himself acknowledged that the old hatred between the two brothers was the main thing stirring their descendents against each other after such a long, long time!

CASE 2: SON CONTESTING/TRAMPLING ON THE FATHER'S AUTHORITY

In 1 Samuel, chapters 2 to 4, the sons of Eli did not pay any respect to their father's authority, which resulted in the following:

Israel lost the war against the Philistines in spite of the presence of the Ark (1 Sam 4:11).
(By the way, this is a classic case of lack of separation unto God from Eli: although he was a God-fearing father, he failed to take a firm stand for the Lord, while his sons were defiling the Temple of God!)

The whole family was decimated on the same day, clearly God's judgment -Father and two sons, plus one wife, who died delivering a baby (1 Sam 2:34, 1Sam 4:17-20) - plus a curse on their clan: they will die young (1Sam2:32)

CASE 3: WOMEN DESPISING THE AUTHORITY OF THEIR HUSBANDS AND OF GOD

JEZEBEL

In 1 Kings 18 the prophet Elijah confronted the false prophets and God glorified Himself in the eyes of the whole nation. In one move, Elijah got rid of all the false prophets in the land, and succeeded in bringing revival to Israel, as all, including King Ahab, proclaimed: *"The Lord is God! The Lord is God! (1 Kings 18:39)"*

The very next day, Jezebel, King Ahab's wife, annulled the whole matter, rebelling against her husband's pledge to serve the true God, by declaring Elijah "wanted dead or alive" (1 Kings 19:2). Finally, she pulled her husband back into his sins, leading to the extermination of the whole dynasty and family of King Ahab (1 Kings 21:21-29, 2 Kings 9 and 2 Kings 10).

MICHAL

She despised King David as he was glorifying God with his dance (2 Sam 6:20). The Bible concludes:

Therefore Michal the daughter of Saul had no children to the day of her death (2 Sam 6:23).

CASE 4: HEADS OF FAMILIES DESPISING GOD'S AUTHORITY:

KORAH, DATHAN AND ABIRAM

These three led a rebellion against God's Authority, and as a consequence, they were destroyed with all their respective families (Numbers 16:31-34).

As Paul insisted in 1 Corinthians 10:11:

These things happened to them as examples and were written down as warnings for us, on whom the culmination of the ages has come.

KING JEROBOAM

He rebelled against God by building golden calves for Israel to worship; his whole dynasty was decimated. (1 K 14:10)

ANANIAS AND SAPPHIRA

As husband and wife, they conspired to lie and thereby to test the Holy Spirit; both fell dead on the same day (Acts 5:9-10)

As a summary:

In any Church system, when at any level there is no submission to the authority of God, either through sin or false doctrine, there is trouble.

Every governing system, where there is no fear of God, leads its nation into trouble.

Finally, when at any level of a family, people don't fear God, or when the chain of submission is broken, disaster is guaranteed.

THE CONCEPT OF FUNCTIONAL AUTHORITY APPLIES IN ALL THREE BRANCHES

Ephesians 5:22-25 speaks about the order and the rules concerning the family:

In reality, the rules begin in verse 21 which says: *"Submit to one another out of reverence for Christ".*

There is a general rule of submission to one another. So despite the fact that the husband is the authority, husband and wife must primarily be in submission to the general law of Christianity, which is to be in submission to each other.

So how do you get it all together?
It is a matter of functional authority. Again, let's go to the civil social authority and see how it works!

During his term, President Bush paid a visit to Mt. Airy, Maryland—a small city in Carroll County, just 30 minutes away from Westminster, where we lived—for some kind of a ceremony. According to the protocol, the President was welcomed into the state by the Governor of Maryland. The party of officials proceeded into Carroll County where they were then welcomed by its Commissioners, culminating in their arrival and welcome into the Town of Mt. Airy by its Mayor.

The interesting thing is that even though the President is the Chief Executive of the United States, he is still subject to the laws of the land, from the State level all the way down to the local level of a small town and therefore, he yields to the authority of the town Mayor!

The same applies to the Governor, County Commissioners, and on down. In fact, at this one occasion, all the levels of government were present, yet none of them was exempt from the laws set forth.

As a matter of fact, at this particular event, President Bush was a Republican, the Governor of Maryland was a Democrat, the President of Carroll County was a Republican and the Mayor of Mount Airy was a Republican. So, it's not a matter of party, it's just a matter of order, and things work like this on a daily basis in the United States.

In any good company, when the president of the company goes to visit a department, although he is the "Big Boss" of the company, he still yields to the authority of the CEO, who welcomes him; and both, in turn, yield for a time to the authority of that department's head, and so on. This is how things work and very well at that!

The same applies in the Church. One day the Vice president of our Central Headquarters visited our local Church in Westminster. While there, we invited him to kindly attend one of our Marriage seminars that happened to be held 10 miles away in the city of Taneytown. In response, he said:

"If your Pastor agrees, I will go! Otherwise, I will not."

On the ladder of Authority, he was at least six to seven steps above our local Pastor, yet, while he was in our city, the rule of Functional Authority applied, and he was in submission to our local Church authority.

FUNCTIONAL AUTHORITY IN A MARRIAGE

What are we saying? The same law applies in marriage.

Prayerfully, we have learned that in a marriage, the functional authority applies to three categories:

The first is the social acceptance that the wife, when it comes to interior things (cooking, household, etc) has the final say.

That authority is recognized by society; therefore, husbands ought to submit joyfully to their wives in this domain and usually do.

Secondly, for example, the Bible says in 1 Corinthians 7:4:

For the wife does not have [exclusive] authority and control over her own body, but the husband [has his rights]; likewise also the husband does not have [exclusive] authority and control over his body, but the wife [has her rights]. (Amplified Bible)

In other words, you, as a husband, have the functional authority over your wife's body, and you as a wife have the functional authority over your husband's body.

The minute you get married, you should yield that authority in all aspects of your married life.

The first aspect, of course, pertains to sexual life. Among the most common problems encountered in marriages, sexual life is amazingly the taboo subject.

Most of the time during our seminars, we literally almost have to squeeze it out of participants; yet the truth is that the majority of couples some way, somehow, have problems in their sexual life, and the main cause is one of the partners refusing his/her body to the other or, worse, using it as some kind of a "psychological" bargaining tool.

Let's say it loud and clear: the whole matter of marriage is all about love and harmony, therefore you should not use the above verse to abuse the situation, particularly if your spouse, for whatever reason (fatigue, sickness, age etc.), cannot perform up to your demands.

Yet you should be aware that, in general, except God in heaven knows that you are momentarily unable to perform, refusing yourself to your spouse is violating the laws of functional authority given by God to your spouse over your body.

The authority of your spouse over your body goes well beyond sexual life, as it is written:

"...watch... over one another" (Heb10:24-Ampl. Bible),

and of course,

"the two will become one"

Clothing: We cannot count how many times we have dressed-up! In the car, ready to go, one of us says:

"that wear of yours does not fit,
I don't like it; please go and change".

We have learned throughout to know that this is also another clear domain where functional authority applies.

Eating: Through the years we have come to know how sweet it is to watch over each other's weight and eating habits, stepping in, all in love, every time a boundary is being crossed, and it has worked very well.

Bodywise: In general, the rule is simple: I (Roger) am her glory, she (Vicky) is my glory; I love her, she loves me; why resist when she is taking care of her glory by asking me to do something to look better, to be and to feel better?

All our friends know the drill: whenever they compliment any of us on our clothing or physical form, the answer is always the same:

"Glory be to God, but go congratulate my spouse!"

These are the two examples showing that some functional authority has been given to the wife. In such domains, in spite of the fact that the man is the supreme authority in the family, he should behave like President Bush in Mt. Airy. Whenever he is in the domain of her functional authority, he should yield to her authority on how to proceed.

The third category of functional authority is God-given ability. When God gives a special gift or a special talent to one of the spouses, most often, particularly when the other does not have it, that is an indication of functional authority. The other is called to submit in that domain to the one chosen, in all harmony.

FUNCTIONAL AUTHORITY IN MARRIAGE: THE EXAMPLE OF SAMSON'S PARENTS

In Judges 13 from verse 2, the Bible gives a very special story:

A certain man of Zorah, named Manoah, from the clan of the Danites, had a wife who was childless, unable to give birth. The angel of the LORD appeared to her and said, "You are barren and childless, but you are going to become pregnant and give birth to a son. Now see to it that you drink no wine or other fermented drink and that you do not eat anything unclean. You will become pregnant and have a son whose head is never to be touched by a razor because the boy is to be a Nazirite, dedicated to God from the womb. He will take the lead in delivering Israel from the hands of the Philistines." Then the woman went to her husband and told him, "A man of God came to me. He looked like an angel of God, very awesome. I didn't ask him where he came from, and he didn't tell me his name. But he said to me, 'You will become pregnant and have a son. Now then, drink no wine or other fermented drink and do not eat any-

thing unclean, because the boy will be a Nazirite of God from the womb until the day of his death.'" Then Manoah prayed to the LORD: "Pardon your servant, Lord. I beg you to let the man of God you sent to us come again to teach us how to bring up the boy who is to be born." God heard Manoah, and the angel of God came again to the woman while she was out in the field; but her husband Manoah was not with her. The woman hurried to tell her husband, "He's here! The man who appeared to me the other day!" Manoah got up and followed his wife. When he came to the man, he said, "Are you the man who talked to my wife?" "I am," he said. So Manoah asked him, "When your words are fulfilled, what is to be the rule that governs the boy's life and work?" The angel of the LORD answered, "Your wife must do all that I have told her. She must not eat anything that comes from the grapevine, nor drink any wine or other fermented drink nor eat anything unclean. She must do everything I have commanded her." Manoah said to the angel of the LORD, "We would like you to stay until we prepare a young goat for you." The angel of the LORD replied, "Even though you detain me, I will not eat any of your food. But if you prepare a burnt offering, offer it to the LORD." (Manoah did not realize that it was the angel of the LORD.) Then Manoah inquired of the angel of the LORD, "What is your name, so that we may honor you when your word comes true?" He replied, "Why do you ask my name? It is beyond understanding." Then Manoah took a young goat, together with the grain offering, and sacrificed it on a rock to the LORD. And the LORD did an amazing thing while Manoah and his wife watched: As the flame blazed up from the altar toward heaven, the angel of the LORD ascended in the flame. Seeing this, Manoah and his wife fell with their faces to the ground. When the angel of the LORD did not show himself again to Manoah and his wife, Manoah realized that it was the angel of the LORD. "We are doomed to die!" he said to his wife. "We have seen God!" But his wife answered, "If the LORD had meant to kill us, he would not have accepted a burnt offering and grain offering from our hands, nor shown us all these things or now told us this."

The Bible states that Manoah and his wife both feared God. But somehow, God (at least temporarily) gave the wife the gift and authority of Prophecy manifested by the ability to receive God's message. Let's take a closer look at their respective attitudes towards that prestigious power given her:

AT THE ANGEL'S FIRST APPEARANCE

Wife:

She realized immediately the immensity of the gift of the word of God awarded her (and not to her husband) over the most important prayer topic they had: the long-awaited baby was on its way.

<u>She said nothing to the angel of God;</u>

Instead she went directly to the husband, to the Authority, to report the fact.

She showed <u>humility</u> in handling that immense privilege from God: She could have easily bragged about her spiritual gifts and taken an inspired position of *"thus says the Lord..."* instead, she instinctively knew what Apostle Paul proclaimed thousands years later:

What are you boasting about?
What have you that you did not receive?"

Again coming from a secular example, imagine an ambassador sent to a foreign country. While there, he is met with an unexpected opportunity for the good of his country, outside his mission description.

Question: Does he go ahead to pull off the deal, sign it, and bring the signed contract back to his president? No! At the very least, he will first report to his authority and receive his instructions, no matter how urgent and attractive the deal is!

That is what Manoah's wife did. She first reported it to her authority! As she proved later on when Manoah feared to die, she was mature enough to know that this was God speaking to her. Yet, when reporting to her husband, she took the lowly position of pulling her husband into the action and having him seek confirmation for himself:

"He looked like the Angel of God"...

In other words she was saying:

I believe he was an Angel of God, but I could be wrong; why don't you go praying for confirmation?

Manoah

Apparently a man of prayer, his reaction was like:

How come it is you, my wife, who received from God for such an important matter? God knows I am the authority; it cannot be the Angel of God, probably just a Man of God. (Note verses 16: and 22).

And so he prayed for confirmation!
And God answered his prayer! The Angel of God appeared a second time… to the wife! Again!

AT THE ANGEL'S SECOND APPEARANCE

Wife:

This time, she did not even wait for him to speak: Again, she did not say a word to the Angel of God, but went directly to call her husband, something like:

"I want you to have the exalted position of bringing the prophecy to our home, straight from God."

Manoah:

Of course, overjoyed, he ran while probably happy inside. So he asked the Angel of God:

"Are You the Man who spoke to this woman?"

His body language was probably something like:

"By the way, how come you spoke directly to my wife when I am the man, the authority?"

So one can imagine his heart sinking inside when the angel told him:

Your wife must do all that I have told her.

Or otherwise:

"She really received by grace the gift of this message,
not you; she is the one to execute it,
you will be just her assistant!"

Manoah was probably very downcast, his ego very much bruised and bleeding inside, but he remembered the laws of hospitality, eventually still clinging to one last hope that he was just a Man of God, not the Angel of the Lord!

So when he saw the miracle of the Angel rising into the smoke, the whole thing (and probably his sin of unbelief) hit him full blast: *"we are going to die"*

Wife:

Then the wife hit a home run: She did not get angry at him for doubting her gift, she did not brag about the outcome proving her right, she did not rejoice over the shame for her husband to now have to submit to her in all due respect in the matter of that prophecy, she simply took her perfect, natural place-the helper fit, reassuring- and in one last stand of humility, instead of admonishing him with:

"thus says the Lord: you shall not die",

she rather moved into the logical and legalistic paradigm of her beloved husband:

"if God wanted us to die, why do all this then kill us?"

KEYS TO A SUCCESSFUL FUNCTIONAL AUTHORITY BASED ON A SPECIAL GIFT OR TALENT

This precious passage emphasizes on the keys to a successful functional authority based on a special gift or talent:

-It's only a functional authority; never forget who the Authority in your home is.
-As much as possible, involve your spouse to have a proactive role in the exercise of your gift.
-It is a free gift from God, received by grace: no one reason to boast.
-Humility toward the other is the central key to success.
-The earlier you identify your spouse's exceptional gifts and submit to them, the better you're off. Resistance will only guarantee that, as with Manoah, God will humble and sometimes humiliate you until you accept His sovereign gift of grace to your spouse.

ROGER

"In our case, God gave my Darling a great sense of stewardship and of management of money. In that field I acknowledge her authority. It was not always that easy, though!

I fell into this trap many times: In my attempt to prove myself as the Authority, I made a few financial decisions against my Darling's advice which turned out to be disasters for our family. Believe me, I've learned the hard way!

It doesn't have to be like that. Please, be proactive, encourage and help your spouse blossom in his/her special gift or talent; you're the winner all the way."

A couple should sit down and make an honest assessment

of all the talents and gifts in each other. Whenever any of them has an exceptional talent or gift, this is an indication from God that in this domain, he/she must be the functional authority and he/she must have the final say.

There is no rule per se, but a couple should be honest in recognizing those gifts and talents, because God has given us those things for our best interest.

IN EACH BRANCH, PROMOTION COMES FROM WITHIN, NOT WITHOUT!

SOCIAL BRANCH

The society has long recognized the crucial sensitivity of promotion; therefore it's a trivia that every social organization in the modern world has its own rules, laws and patterns for promotion:

Every good company, every good association, has its by-laws and internal rules stating how promotion must be made at all levels of its organization.

Every local government is in charge of organizing, within its own locality, elections at all levels for their top executives, who, in turn, can promote officials according to local rules and laws.

At the state or federal level, the same goes: the existing governing body has the charge of organizing the elections for all its top executives, within its own territory of authority.

Even in a Monarchy, every ruling dynasty has established clear rules on how the next king will be chosen.

The recent history of the United Kingdom gives vivid

examples of such: many times the world has learned that a prince, clearly qualified to be the next king, has opted out of kingship by knowingly violating the existing rules of succession.

In every single country in which those promotion rules have been violated at any level (coup, manipulations, etc…), there has been chaos.

On the other hand, throughout History, and recently in many developing countries, whenever there was a vacancy at the top executive level without a clear, transparent process for promoting a new leader from within, there has been chaos.

SPIRITUAL BRANCH

Most Church systems have by-laws for promoting leaders at all levels from within.

Whenever such a clear process was missing, there was chaos in case of vacancy.

FAMILY BRANCH

Therefore, any promotion in the family should be from within the familial branch. Biblical examples:

As head of the family, **Jacob** destituted Ruben from elder son (Gen 49:4), and promoted Joseph, his tenth son, as the new leader of the family (Gen 49:26).

The same **Jacob**, played his elder brother Esau and bought his birthright from him (Gen 25:29); however he knew very well, as did Rebecca his mother, that <u>the deal had no value until their father Isaac validates it by giving Jacob the blessing reserved for the elder of the children</u>, which he and Rebecca tricked Isaac into doing (Gen 27:35).

Ruth, upon returning with her Mother-in-law back to Israel, knew that her promotion within the family had to come from the sole familial authority left to her, Naomi.

Therefore she left the whole matter into her hands and merely executed to the letter every prescription she received from Naomi (Ruth 2:22; Ruth 3:1-4); as a reward, she was promoted from the rank of a Moabite (not even allowed in the assembly of God (Deut 23:3)), to being the wife of one of the mightiest men in town (Ruth4:13), to being the grandmother of King David, and one of the ancestors of the Lord Jesus-Christ (Matt 1:5).

SOME BIBLICAL EXAMPLES OF VIOLATIONS

King Jeroboam (1 Kings 12:29-31): As King, he decided as well to become the spiritual leader of Israel, not only imposing what people should worship, but also appointing priests who were not according to the established process (the law was that spiritual leaders had to belong to the tribe of the Levites).

As a consequence, Israel fell into a spiritual slump from which the Nation never recovered until the Deportation.

King Uzziah (2 Chron 26 :16-21) : He promoted himself to the priest position and entered the temple in order to perform duties reserved to priests only. He came instantly under God's judgment, and was a leper from that time for the rest of his life.

Athaliah (2 Chron 11) : Upon hearing that Ahaziah king of Judah, had suddenly died, being the king's mother, she attempted to transfer her authority from the family branch into the social branch:

She violated the existing process (of letting the elders of Judah appoint and anoint one of the King's children as the new Leader), and after destroying all potential candidates, she proclaimed herself queen of Judah

Immediately, confusion was in the land, to the point that she was herself killed after a plot led by Jehoiada the high priest, who immediately restored the regular process.

Miriam, the elder sister of Moses, also tried to make a transfer of her familial authority into competing with Moses in the spiritual Branch (Numbers 12:2).

As a result, she incurred God's judgment and was a leper for seven days (Numbers 12:10-15)

SO, WHO'S WHO IN THE MARRIAGE PROCESS?

Marriage is definitely one promotion within the family branch, and no doubt, the Bible confers authority for this matter to the head of the family branch as confirmed throughout the Scriptures with the marriage of Isaac (Gen 24:4), Jacob (Gen 28:2), Ruth cited above, Samson (Judges 14:2-4), etc…

Paul said to the Corinthians:

So also then, he [the father] who gives his virgin (his daughter) in marriage does well, and he [the father] who does not give [her] in marriage does better
(1 Cor 7:38- Amplified Bible).

This passage clearly establishes that the marriage decision process (namely "whether to get married" and "to whom to get married"), belongs to the familial authority.

Going back to the diagram on the familial branch of God's authority, let us revisit the notion of marriage per 1 Cor 11:3:

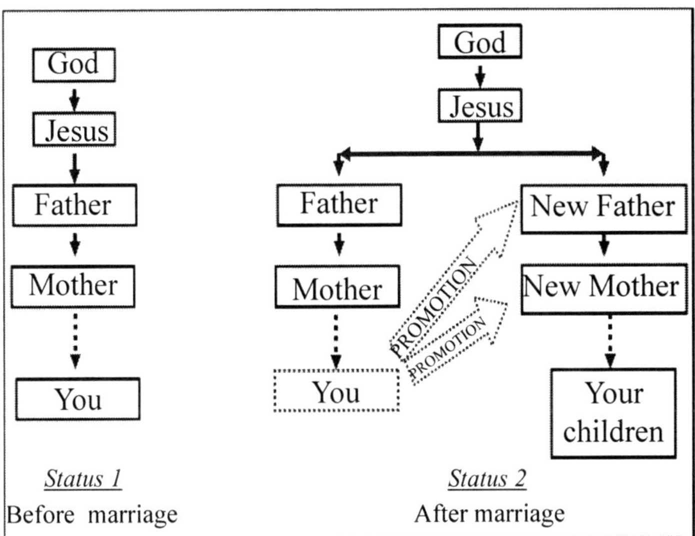

Indeed, when you get married, it is as if God just created a new department in His Kingdom and put you in charge, so that the same verse (1 Cor 11:3) may now apply directly to you; you are now entrusted with a new department, as new Father, or new Mother, with subsequent shift in the direct Authority over you:

As a newlywed husband, within your own family branch you are no longer under your Father and Mother's authority, but directly under God's Authority through Jesus-Christ!

Let it be said loud and clear: this new status of yours, by no means, exempts you from the commandment: you must still and always honor Father and Mother.

As a newlywed wife, within your own family branch, you are no longer under your Father and Mother's Authority, but you have been transferred directly under your husband's authority; once again let it be said loud and clear: this new status of yours, by no means, exempts you from the commandment: you must still and always honor Father and Mother.

Both of you, newlywed husband and wife, now have the final word on your own family matters; yet, in all meetings and other matters of your initial family, each of you should still submit to your Father and Mother.

You, parents of the newlywed, are now in the position of a president retiring from politics, who battled campaign for the next president from your own party, and got him elected: True, he owes you a lot; true your counselling to him is priceless; true, your experience is invaluable for him to succeed.

Question: Does that mean that you now have the right to intrude in his government at will, to make decisions in his place within his government?

You, parents of the newlywed are now in the position of a head of department who took one good employee, trained him well, and then recommended him to be hired as the new head of another department, so that both of you are now under the direct orders of the same Vice President in your company: that makes colleagues. One more time: True, he owes you a lot; true, your counselling to him is priceless, true, your experience is invaluable for him to succeed.

Question: Does that mean that you now have the right to intrude in his department at will, to override his decisions in his department?

Of course, the answers are no, and this illustration gives a new perspective to the need of being separated upon marriage!

WHAT AUTHORITY DOES THE SOCIAL BRANCH HAVE IN THE MARRIAGE PROCESS?

For reasons of public order and security, as well as provision, which are its primary mandate in God's pattern of Authority over us, the social branch has the right to legislate and secure the bond of marriage. Again, every obedience is and must always be "unto the Lord", therefore, it is always a blessing to submit to the social prescriptions, as long as they do not go against the word of God!

SO WHAT IS THE PLACE OF THE CHURCH IN THIS PROCESS?

A great one!

The Church has the eternal duty of the expansion of God's Kingdom, namely to counsel and bless all activities of its members, including marriage.

The Church has the eternal authority to intervene to guide and teach believers, including those preparing for marriage, on the ways of the Lord, and particularly, to help them live a holy life, to warn them against sinful ways and the snares of the enemy.

The Bible gives the Church the authority to make sure its member marries a believer (1 Cor 7:39, 2 Cor 6:14-18).

As we said earlier, when it comes down to who will decide if and with whom a member should marry, that authority is biblically given to the family authority. However, the Church has the duty of counselling, prayer and intercession all along the whole process.

We know a few Christian Churches in which by-laws had to be changed to set Parental Approval as the first pre-requisite in the process of Church involvement in organizing a wedding. Why? Because, after many decades of existence, their own statistics had spoken loud and clear: Of all marriages in which

1) the parental authorities were opposed, and

2) the Church authorities had approved,

not one had worked. Not one! And this, for one good reason: the commandment with a promise says:

"Honor your father and mother ... so that things will go well for you, and you will live for a long time in the land. (Eph 2:2- Common English Bible)

THE DELICATE MATTER OF CHOOSING YOUR MARRIAGE PARTNER

The big question is: who has authority in choosing your marriage partner? From the chapter above, at least we know who has not: neither the Social, nor the spiritual branch!

Now therefore, in the family branch, who has the final word over the choice of your marriage partner?

First, we repeat one more time that all branches of authority can, and usually do interact in terms of advice, counselling, warning against sin or a trap you did not see, etc…

Let's consider the case (not so rare!) of a person in conflict with the family, and sometimes others, on the choice of a spouse.

First, The Bible is clear: Eph 5: 25 says:

Husbands, love your wives...

The man must love his wife! That settles the issue: only the bridegroom can determine his feelings, nobody else! Therefore, whatever the process, the final word belongs to the person getting married, and therefore, as long as he does not feel love, it is a no!

Besides, the Bible comes to his rescue:

Fathers, do not irritate and provoke
your children to anger (Eph6:4)

Secondly, the main verse concerning the involvement of the familial authority is in Eph 6:2-3

"Honor your father and mother ...
so that things will go well for you,
and you will live for a long time in the land.
(Eph 6:2-3 Common English Bible)

And the key word is "honor". It is a commandment; therefore, the choice of your partner, just like any endeavour of yours, must honor Father and Mother for blessings to flow.

That is a spiritual law, and, says the Bible,
Let God be true, and every human being a liar! (Rom 3:4)
There is just no way around it! Parents must be honored in the process of choosing your marriage partner!

This is where the notion of "honoring the Parents" comes into the picture.

HONORING THE PARENTS: THE WAY OF SURE BLESSINGS

There is no universal standard for honoring the parents, because it goes with culture, and sometimes even within a given culture, it may vary with individual families.

Only one thing is certain: in the process of choosing your marriage partner, the family authorities must be honored; based on our experience, we can sort out 4 main categories:

THE WESTERN AND EUROPEAN CULTURE

The majority of parents in the Western culture have made up their minds that, once at adult age, their child may choose to marry the person of his/her choice, so they do not feel dishonored when this happens with zero input from the family authorities.

Their sense of honor tends more to be whether or not their child's general behavior is in line with the values they taught him/her, including marriage matters. Also, they feel honored if they have a part to play in the actual organization of the wedding.

That's the easiest place to honor parents. In such cases, most of the times, all you have to do to honor them is to involve them in the ceremony!

ASIAN, MIDDLE EAST AND AFRICAN CULTURES

In these cultures, the family bonds are generally very strong; therefore, to various degrees, there is almost always a cultural process involving part or the whole family, for choosing the marriage partner, and/or for accepting the proposal, and/or for organizing the wedding, all this rooted in traditions.

Most of the time, families feel dishonored when those steps (again which vary from place to place) are by-passed, rejected or ignored.

With modernity knocking at the door, many cultures have evolved substantially to reduce the burden of such traditions to a minimum. However, the remaining processes are still enforced in many places. We have seen many Christian couples literally "negotiate" their way through those processes, trying to find compromises to keep everybody happy, in order to obtain their blessing. Smart move!

LATIN AMERICAN CULTURES

"Honoring the parents" in theses cultures is generally a mix of the two preceding categories, as their populations are mostly made of people from European, Amerindian and black African backgrounds, the vast majority overall being those of mixed White-Native and White-Black races.

The degree of mixing varies, with extremes like Uruguay, Argentina and Costa Rica having more than 80% of Europeans, Haiti being made of 95% blacks, while Bolivia and Guatemala have a majority of Amerindians, and all the rest have various degrees of mixes in-between.

CROSSOVERS OR THE CLASH OF CULTURES

Many young Christians are caught in the middle, generally those living in or according to the Western world, and yet, having their parents still rooted in their traditions.

Many a time, those youths revolt against those traditions and just "do their thing". Not smart: by so doing, before God they violated the Precious Commandment and most of the time, such couples are not blessed in the long run. From experience, we recommend the following:

GENERAL ROADMAP TO SUCCESS

There is no clear-cut formula, only principles:

-Family authorities must be honored, that is clear. Talk to your parents; make sure you understand their own perception of honor in your marriage process.

-As long as there is nothing sinful in the process, the best way is by far to submit, you can only be blessed!

-When honoring the family authorities requires that you commit a sin (like idol worship, libations to other gods, etc...), the best way is to prayerfully negotiate your way out of it, claiming your Christian values, and sometimes using mediations, including bringing along your pastors, who are generally highly respected even among unbelievers. God will move, guaranteed! It is just a matter of time!

-Sometimes, also involve the Church in the spiritual battle in such tough cases.

Once we had a sister in our worship team; her mother, who was very attached to pagan religious rites, had sworn that she would never accept to give her daughter to one of those "Jesus-alleluias", as she called Christians.

Sure enough, the sister fell in love with a brother in the Church who wanted to marry her; and sure enough, the mother dismissed them, swearing "never, ever" to accept a Christian son-in-law. After one year of waiting, prayerfully, we were led to organize a chain-fasting for their marriage: two people would fast for each day of the week, week in and week out, until victory.

The morning after the 52nd day, the mother called her daughter and, just like that, said: "Can you tell your fiancé that I want to see him?" Of course, she ran to call him. When the brother arrived, she said in substance: "I cannot tell you why, but since a few days, I came to realize that everything has been crumbling in my life lately, and, the way I see it, it all began from the day when I rejected you as my in-law; ok, I now accept you as my son, you can marry my daughter, and I will bless both of you".
Glory be to God!!!

TRUE SERVICE OF GOD IS DAILY SUBMISSION IN ALL THREE BRANCHES OF GOD'S AUTHORITY.

Every situation, every passage calling for the role of the wife, of the husband, of the children in the family always says something like "as in the Lord", "as obeying the Lord", "according to the Lord", etc.

The same thing goes for the second branch of authority. Ephesians 6 (Amplified Bible) continues with how things should be functioning with regard to workers and their bosses:

Servants (slaves), be obedient to those who are
your physical masters, having respect for them
and eager concern to please them, in singleness of motive
and with all your heart, as [service] to Christ [Himself]--
Not in the way of eye-service [as if they were watching you]
and only to please men, but as servants (slaves) of Christ,
doing the will of God heartily and with your whole soul;
Rendering service readily with goodwill,
as to the Lord and not to men,
Knowing that for whatever good anyone does,
he will receive his reward from the Lord,
whether he is slave or free.
You masters, act on the same [principle] toward them
and give up threatening and using violent
and abusive words, knowing that
He Who is both their Master and yours
is in heaven, and that there is no respect of persons
(no partiality) with Him.

The Bible is clear that in the social branch, boss or servant, we are to work "as for the Lord", not for a man.

The service is for God!

In summary:

While you are doing your duties within the family as unto God, you are serving God.

You should be submitted to the authority of your father and mother in the family as a part of submission to God.

Resisting your boss at work is resisting God; resisting your governor is resisting God.

Submitting to spiritual authorities, of course, is submitting to God. This is the type of "submission to God" that most people know about! But the truth is, this one is only a portion of the whole picture.

IT'S ALL ABOUT THE LOVE OF GOD FOR YOU:

Your family is the outstretched arm of God's love for care, early provision, upbringing and preparation for adult life. Then, when you are promoted to create your own family, it becomes the perfect place for you and your spouse to pass on God's love to your offspring.

Your boss and the entire social branch above him and you, represent the extended hand of God's love for your emotional and social well-being, provision, security and protection.

And of course, the spiritual Authority is the sweet and reassuring voice of God to lead you safely in His Love Branches, and to blend it all together.

GOD'S BLESSINGS FLOW FROM TOP TO BOTTOM TO REACH YOU!

God has laid all your blessings in the hands of the authorities above you, according to Heb7:7

Yet it is beyond all contradiction that it is the lesser person who is blessed by the greater one.

This applies to all branches of God's authority.

Family authority

Ephesians 6:1-3 says:

Children, obey your parents in the Lord, for this is right.
"Honor your father and mother," which is
the first commandment with promise: "that it may be
well with you and you may live long on the earth."

Deuteronomy 27:16:

Cursed is he who dishonors his father or his mother
(amplified Bible)

It is like a coin: On one side you have the blessings, if you choose to honor your parents; on the other side, it is a curse, if you choose to dishonor them.

Then, as we said before, the same rules extend to the other branches of God's authority.

Social authority

In Deuteronomy 33, the whole passage is about Moses, then the undisputed leader, blessing the Children of Israel.

In 1 Kings 8:55, King Solomon blessed the Assembly.

As stated above, throughout the Scriptures, the fate and blessings of the nation generally depended entirely on the spiritual standing of the reigning king: Blessings whenever the King feared God, trouble and doom when he did not walk with the Lord.

On the other hand, Paul repeated in Acts 23:5 what Moses had laid out in Exodus 22:28:

" Do not speak evil about the ruler of your people."

Spiritual authority

In Numbers 6:22-27, God told Moses to give the charge of blessing Israel to the Priests Aaron and his sons.

At the end of the day, it all comes down to the submission to the family authority for many reasons:

The commandment is for the family first, then is extended to the other branches, because Family is the perfect place to teach obedience, to train a child in submission to authorities; he will just transport it as he grows, to the other branches of God's authority, as said in Proverbs 22:6

Train up a child in the way he should go,
And when he is old he will not depart from it.

Training a child to submit to and honor his parents will automatically make him to submit to and honor all authorities in his life. In fact, statistics prove that the great majority of the children who are in jail, in trouble and other facilities for juvenile crime come from disturbed and destructed families where this flow of authority has been broken.

On the other hand, it is not by coincidence if the official statistics prove clearly that the ones coming from stable families, with Father and Mother in a healthy marriage, have a much, much greater chance to never undergo such havocs(*4)

For this reason, we usually sum it up in our marriage counselling by the following bold declaration:

"All your blessings depend on your relationship
with your Father and Mother"

WHAT HAPPENS WHEN OBEDIENCE MEANS SIN AGAINST GOD?

Again, we must honor the authority, and there is no debate over that. We have no right to ridicule the authority!

The Bible gives the example of Peter and John when they were given the order by the Sanhedrin to disobey the Word of God:

"*But Peter and John replied: Judge for yourself whether it is right in God's sight to obey you rather than God".*
(Acts 4:19)

They did not disrespect the Sanhedrin. They just stood by God's side and humbly spoke to the Sanhedrin in all due respect, calling upon their own conscience and good sense. This is what we should do.

Whenever confronted with family, work, and sometimes Church (false doctrine, false or deceived believer, honest mistake, etc.), if anyone in Authority asks you to go against the Word of God, the Bible gives you the right, in all due respect and honor, to tell the person:

"I recognize your authority; I honor you as my boss, as my father, as my mother, as my spiritual authority, etc.; but I'm sorry, the Word of God says the opposite of what you are asking me to do. With all due respect, judge for yourself whether it is right in God's sight to obey you rather than God".

You've got to avoid the scandal, but honor the person.

IN CONCLUSION

Yes to the fourth law of Marriage is a "Yes" to accepting the following **root change**:

Submission to righteous instructions within my family branch is submission to God.

Submitting to my boss at work, to my governor and president through obedience to the righteous laws of the land is submitting to God.

Submitting to my pastor and spiritual leader in the Church is submitting to God.

And on the other hand, rebelling against them is creating a schism, a civil war:

In the family first,
At my job site, second;
And in the Church, third.

Yes to Law No.4, the Law of Submission means:

"Yes Lord, I acknowledge from now on, that the extended hand of God's blessing and love over me goes through:

My father, my mother and my elder siblings, that You have placed as familial authorities above me;

my boss or school officials, my Mayor, Governor, President and other officials that You gave me as social authorities;

as well as my spiritual authorities, that You gave me to blend it all together!

Praise be to Your holy Name, amen!

CHAPTER V

YES TO LAW N°5: THE LAW OF THE BODY

ROGER

"It was somewhere around May or June 1995. My Darling had traveled to another city for a short family visit, and I was home alone with our kids. That day while I was meditating the Word of God, I just fell on Ephesians 5 beginning in verse 25:

"Husbands love your wives just as Christ loved the Church and gave himself up for her. In the same way, husbands ought to love their wives as their own bodies. He who loves his wife loves himself. After all, no one ever hated his own body. But he treats and cares for it just as Christ does for the Church."

At that moment, for the first time in my Christian life, I distinctly heard the Voice of the Lord speaking to me in my spirit:

"My son."

"Yes Lord", I answered.

"Roll up the shirt sleeve on your right arm and look at your wrist."

I obeyed.

"What do you see?"

"I see an old scar."

"Do you remember how you got this scar?"

"Yes Lord, I remember distinctly it was somewhere around June or July 1981 in New Orleans, Louisiana in the USA."

"What happened?"

"My car was overheating, and I needed to add some water to the radiator. As I opened the radiator cap, suddenly water vapor blasted onto my wrist and bubbles began to appear: big, big bubbles full of water!"

"Let me ask you a few questions: Was it painful?"

"Oh yes Lord, it was very, very painful!"

"How did you treat the arm: did you insult it?"

"No Lord."

"Did you curse it?"

"No Lord, I didn't."

"Did you condemn it?"

"No Lord, I didn't."

"What did you do?"

"I went immediately to the doctor to get it treated."

"When you got to the doctor, did you accuse the arm?"

"Nooo!!"

"In short, did you treat the arm with more or less care than when it's not hurting you?"

"Much more care!"

"Hold that right arm with your left hand."

I did. The Lord continued:

"This right arm is your wife, Vicky. And every time she hurts you for whatever reason, on purpose or not, this passage that you just read means that your right arm is hurting, you just got a burn; treat her exactly the way you treated that arm on that day."

Then the Spirit left and I came back to my senses.

Wow…!!

I mean, it was THE revelation that changed my whole vision of marriage—A life-changing experience! That was the most wonderful dynamic encounter with God, as my pastor used to call it, in my spiritual life at that point. That happened on a Saturday afternoon; I remember, the next day, when my Darling came back from her short trip, I welcomed her with:

"Honey, our problems are finished!"

She didn't understand, of course, and she said: "What do you mean?" And I shared my meditation, my encounter with the Lord with her. And truly, truly, since that day, our problems are finished. I mean, the Word of God is so alive and so true, and that "one flesh" thing ("the two shall become one flesh") brought all its meaning to us and everything changed".

CONTRACT vs COVENANT

Pastor Francis, who plunged us into the waters of baptism, was the first to teach us this truth:

Many couples see marriage as a contract;
God's vision of marriage is a Covenant (the Lamb and His Bride, the Church, being the heavenly model-Hebrews 8:7-8).
What is the difference between a contract and a covenant?

CONTRACT-MARRIAGE

In general, a contract, among others, is made up of:

Two parties
Each having their own interest
A binding act
Rules of functioning
Termination terms

How do people behave whenever there is a contract?

First everyone is looking out for their own interest: his/her own happiness.

The other is needed only as long as that interest is still valid.

The moment one party is not happy, separation is envisioned.

Each party records all the mistakes and violations of the other party.

Each of them prepares for and anticipates the day of separation (otherwise known as plan B).

That's exactly what we see today: Most marriages are contract-marriages, and we hear more and more about prenuptial contracts. Couples come together anticipating separation, preparing for it-ready for it.

COVENANT-MARRIAGE

In a covenant you'll find:

Two parties blending into one
A common goal
A binding act
Rules of functioning
No time limit
No termination envisioned.

GOD'S VISION OF MARRIAGE IS A COVENANT!

The two are Man and Woman, anything else is abomination (Lev18:22, Rom1:24-27).

The common goal is to take care of the Lord's garden: worship from their hearts in the Spirit and in Truth.

The binding action is the grafting of one into the other

...the two will become one flesh (Mark 10:7)

Once again, making the analogy of the heavenly marriage between the Lamb of God and his Bride, which is the Church, Jesus said in John 15:1:

"I am the vine and you are the branches"

In Romans 11:

If some of the branches have been broken off, and you, though God's wild olive shoot, have been grafted in among the others and God shares in the nourishing sap from the olive root, do not boast over those branches. If you do, consider this: You do not support the root, but the root supports you. You will say then, "Branches were broken off so that I could be grafted in."

In short, God sees marriage as a branch from a given tree grafted into a new tree, and from there, there is no separation; the two live together forevermore.

How?

As one body. Once more, using the Christ-Church analogy to understand God's vision of marriage, 1 Corinthians 13 reads:

12The body is a unit, though it is made up of many parts; and though all its parts are many, they form one body. So it is with Christ. ...14Now the body is not made up of one part but of many. 15If the foot should say, "Because I am not a hand, I do not belong to the body," it would not for that reason cease to be part of the body. 16And if the ear should say, "Because I am not an eye, I do not belong to the body," it would not for that reason cease to be part of the body. 17If the whole body were an eye, where would the sense of hearing be? If the whole body were an ear, where would the sense of smell be? 18But in fact God has arranged the parts in the body, every one of them, just as he wanted them to be. 19If they were all one part, where would the body be? 20As it is, there are many parts, but one body.

21The eye cannot say to the hand, "I don't need you!" And the head cannot say to the feet, "I don't need you!" 22On the contrary, those parts of the body that seem to be weaker are indispensable, 23and the parts that we think are less honorable we treat with special honor. And the parts that are unpresentable are treated with special modesty, 24while our presentable parts need no special treatment. But God has combined the members of the body and has given greater honor to the parts that lacked it, 25so that there should be no division in the body, but that its parts should have equal concern for each other. 26If one part suffers, every part suffers with it; if one part is honored, every part rejoices with it."

HOW DOES THE BODY FUNCTION?

The key word is complementarity: Each part of the body is different and knows its usefulness. Each is unique and has a unique function, even when duplicated, as in hands, feet, toes and fingers.

Perfect coordination is through acknowledging and accepting the leadership of the head: Each member refers to, and is always triggered and directed by the head.

Take the simple action of eating an apple from the table. Let us look closer at the process and break it down to illustrate our point:

All kinds of mechanisms from the stomach, throat, tongue, and the digestive system such as tasting, chewing and swallowing, trigger the desire for food which is transmitted to the head (brain) for action.

The head orders the neck to turn towards the table, and both eyes to focus on the apples. Each part responds and sends information back to the head.

Now the head gives orders to the feet and all the related muscles and body parts to move towards the table, coordinated by the eyes, which tell the head when the apples are within reach.

The head then orders the hand to lay hold of the apple, and after the first screening by the eyes to eliminate the visibly bad ones and choose the best-looking one, the hand brings it to the mouth.

The head activates the smell and taste mechanism through the nose, the tongue and their related parts, which all can immediately inform the head whether the apple is good or bad, sweet or sour, ripe or green, rotten inside or not, etc.

After deeming it safe to eat, the head orders the full mechanism of eating and enjoying the apple, and the invisible digestive parts to take over.

Perfect coordination, perfect harmony, perfect result: Victory for the body.

The principle of the body is well known and well applied in today's society, right before our eyes. Where? In the No.1 media attraction: sports!

Every successful coach knows that the key to victory is to define a clear strategy and prepare his team to apply that strategy as one body, where each plays his role and relates to each teammate as prescribed by the Head Coach.

Usually, the champion team is rarely the one with the most superstars, but rather, time and time again, the one where complementarity and coordination are most perfected, with total obedience to the Head Coach. It's all over the TV, the newspapers, the radio, internet and all media—day in and day out!

Marriage was meant to be the Greatest Team of all, one Body with Man and Woman as parts, with Jesus as the Head (meaning coordinated by God through His Word).

So where do most couples miss it?

THE ONE-FLESH CONCEPT

...the two will become one flesh (Mark 10:7)

In a marriage, once the man or the woman sees and accepts that as husband and wife they are truly one flesh, that settles it! That's what happened to us.
And they truly are one flesh!

In one session, Eddy, accompanied by his wife, asked us what that really meant, so we had the following conversation that, we believe, was the Lord's revelation:
"Eddy, do you believe that Junior, your son, is really one flesh with you?"
"Yes."
"What about him being one flesh with his mother?"
"Absolutely true, he is one flesh with his mother"
"So is Junior one flesh with both you and his mother?"
"Yes, absolutely!"
"No doubt?"
"Not a bit!"
"Now who is Junior for both of you?"
"Our son."
"Or fruitwise?"
"Junior is the fruit of his mother and me."
"Now please open the Bible to Luke 6:44; what do you read?"
(after finding the passage) "*Each tree is recognized by its own fruit!*"
"The Bible is saying that if you see a mango you know it's the fruit of…?"
"…A mango tree."
"If you see a banana you know it's the fruit of…?"
"…A banana tree."

"Therefore, if you see Eddy Jr, who is a one-flesh fruit of his father and mother, what does that make both of you?"
"Gee! A one-flesh tree!"
"Voila, Monsieur!"
"Mind-blowing, yet so simple, and so true! But wait a minute! Why then do so many people divorce?"
"Does that fact change anything to what we shared?"
"You tell me!"
"Ok Eddy, did you ever hear a father say to his son: 'you have done this, you're no longer my son'?"
"Yes, I have!"
"What about a son saying to his Dad: 'You're no longer my father'?"
"Sure!"
"Question: Does it change anything whatsoever to the fact that they remain father and son?"
"Absolutely not."
"Does it change the fact that they are still one flesh? Does the declaration change their DNA?"
"Of course not!"
"Does it remove the fact that he is the one-flesh fruit of the one-flesh tree of the tandem father-mother?"
"Surely not!"
"Why would then a declaration by some humans in a courthouse suddenly change the fact that you and your wife are the one-flesh tree manifested through your one-flesh son?"
"Wow!"
"Besides, dear Eddy, it's even more serious than that; please read 1 Corinthians 6:16."

Do you not know that he who unites himself with a prostitute is one with her in body? For it is said, "The two will become one flesh.

What do you think, Eddy?"
"Oh my! Oh My! That explains why we sometimes find so

many abnormalities in our children that come seemingly from nowhere in the family!"
"Yes!"
"This could be the result of some act of fornication in a distant past! We are actually carrying in us all the people we committed fornication with, into our marriage, into our spouses and into our children!!!"
"Exactly!"
"Oh! The horror of fornication and adultery! It is actually like having spiritual multiple personalities dormant in us, ready to manifest in our offspring! Oh my!"
"That's another reason why every couple needs the Lord Jesus, who, as our redeemer has paid the price at Golgotha and has the power to remove the consequence of our past sins! Praise His name!"

This conversation was the turning point for Eddy and his wife as they fully grasped the concept.

SYNERGY

Another great asset tied to the law of the Body, or the one-flesh concept, is the synergy created.
Difference is Synergy:

The more different a couple is, the richer they are. To use a physical analogy, imagine a couple facing each other: She sees what he cannot see, and he sees what she can't.

Therefore, as one body, a couple can see 360 degrees instead of just 180 degrees individually. Therefore, they have a much larger scope of vision on anything; thus, they are richer!

DIFFERENT?

Of course, women are different from men! Physically, there is no confusion between a man and a woman.

Actually, we are two different species:

The way we think

The way we react to everything from marital, sexual life, what we like, to our whole World view.

We are emotionally, completely different and react differently when facing difficulties, situations, and crises.

We are just different!

Many couples spend time trying to change each other; but actually, many women do not realize they are trying to change their man into a woman and vice versa (of course we mean behavior-wise).

We have heard so many couples saying: "Oh, we have so much in common", which is great.

But when you change your paradigm: seeing that she is you, she is the other part of you, an extension of yourself and vice versa, then everything that she has different from you is a thing that God has given you as extra talent, extra qualifications.

When two people put their energies together to do something, it's always better than the sum of each individual.

That is what is called "synergy".

So many couples spend a lot of time fighting to actually be alike, not realizing that when you are alike, competition starts. Whereas when you are different and when you know that you should be using the synergy of both to blend into one for victory, it's just a better team!

Again, it's like having two more eyes in the back, because she sees what you cannot see, and vice versa, in every situation.

What if all those things over which couples are fighting because they see differently were simply blessings that God has given them to go the extra mile for synergy, leading to victory?

Instead of looking only at what you have in common, why not look also at what you don't have in common and how you can combine them for victory?

To illustrate this synergy idea, we had this conversation with Tom and Ash who were being upset at being so different in many fields:

-Tom, how many talents do you believe that you have?

-About three.

-What about Ash?

-Three talents also.

-Keep in mind, the Bible says that talents are wealth. Ok, suppose you and Ash have exactly the same 3 talents, say talents T1, T2, and T3… Look at this table and tell me: how many possible combinations for riches and blessings do you have?

T1, T2, T3	(3) each talent taken alone
T1T2, T1T3, T2T3	(+3) combined two by two
T1T2T3	(+1) all together
Total:3+3+1=7 possible combinations of riches in talents	

-Seven possible combinations of talents.

-OK! Now look at what you really have if you combine your actual 3 talents to her own; call hers A1, A2 and A3…

What do you get?

T1, T2, T3, A1,A2,A3	(6) each talent alone
T1T2, T1T3, T1A1, T1A2, T1A3, T2T3, T2A1, T2A2, T2A3, T3A1, T3A2, T3A3, A1A2, A1A3, A2A3	(+15) combined two by two
T1T2T3, T1T2A1, T1T2A2, T1T2A3, T1T3A1, T1T3A2, T1T3A3, T2T3A1, T2T3A2, T2T3A3, T3A1A2, T3A1A3, T3A2A3, A1A2A3	(+14) combined 3 by 3
T1T2T3A1,T1T2T3A2,T1T2T3A3, T1T2A1A2, T1T2A1A3, T1T2A2A3, T1T3A1A2, T1T3A1A3, T1T3A2A3, T2T3A1A2,T2T3A1A3,T2T3A2A3, T1A1A2A3,T2A1A2A3 T3A1A2A3	(+15) combined 4 by 4
T1T2T3A1A2,T1T2T3A1A3,T1T2T3 A2A3, T1T2A1A2A3,T1T3A1A2A3, T1T3A1A2A3	(+6) combined 5 by 5
T1T2T3A1A2A3	(+1) all together
Total:6+15+14+15+6+1=57 possible combinations of riches in talents	

-Wow! 6+15+14+15+6+1= a total of 57 possibilities!

More than 8 times!

-Yep!

-All that time wasted, fighting each other instead of counting our blessings!

-I could not have said it better, Tom!

Genesis from 2:19 says:

So the man gave names to all the livestock, the birds of the air and all the beasts of the field. But for Adam no suitable helper was found... The man said, "This is now bone of my bones and flesh of my flesh; she shall be called 'woman, for she was taken out of man." »

Let one thing be clear:
The whole idea of bringing Man and Woman together was all about suitability, therefore likeness; so there is absolutely nothing wrong in having things in common in a married couple. In fact, biblically, it's the real starting point of the attraction leading to love, and it is a very wonderful thing, there is no problem with that.

IT'S ALL ABOUT COMPLEMENTARITY

What we are saying is that on the other hand, God is by no means in the business of duplication when it comes to creation, particularly the creation of human beings: the Lord made sure of at least three things:

-No two human beings, including perfect twins, are exactly the same in everything, no matter how much of "look-alikeness" they have physically.

-No matter how great you are, you can always learn something from any "small" person.

-Whoever you are, there is at least one domain where you are the best in your zone of influence: The only question is to find it.

In fact, from the Genesis of Human kind, the Lord intended Man and Wife to complement each other; (Gen 2 :20)

Many scholars have had scientific evidence that the brains of Man and Woman actually complement each other [(Walter Johnson, eHow Contributor: Male Vs. Female Brain Theory-ttp://www.ehow.com/about_7231636_male-vs_-female-brain-theory.html)]

Therefore each couple should evaluate objectively not only what they have in common, but also the talents and things where they are different, with the one-flesh concept and complementarity in mind, for untold blessings and victory! What a shift!!

IN CONCLUSION,

The key to the Law of the Body is the inner revelation from God of the "One-flesh" concept. This will by no means guarantee a problem-free marriage, but we know by experience the healing power of that revelation.

Root change: Our wish is that, just as it goes with us, every time you, as husband and wife have a quarrel or argument, one of you will always end up reminding the other:

"Honey, why are we fighting? Our problems are finished.
You're aware that I love you; you love me;
and you and I are grafted by the Lord.
In any situation:
Despising you is despising myself.
Humiliating you is humiliating myself.
Honoring you is honoring myself.
Any good that I do to you is a good to myself.
Ridiculing you, is ridiculing myself.
Slandering you is slandering myself.
Gossiping about you is gossiping about myself.
You are me, I am you and that is final!
And nothing will ever change that!
So anytime I do something you don't like,
please remember, it only can be an accident
because I would never, ever plan anything to harm you
or do something to sadden you.
Our problems are finished!"

May the Lord bless you as you receive this revelation, and own it to make it yours. Please, hold the hand of your spouse and just tell him or her:

"Our problems are finished, because you are grafted in me: You are me and I am you, and that's final!"

May God bless you!

CHAPTER VI

YES TO LAW N°6: THE LAW OF TRINITY

ℑ

We'll always remember one particular seminar organized in Yaoundé, Cameroon, with a French guest-speaker. That brother gave us this wonderful revelation, and it was the Lord teaching us the sixth law: The Law of Trinity.

When we say "Trinity", of course, the first thing that comes to mind is the Divine Trinity: Father, Son and Holy Spirit.

DIVINE TRINITY

DIVINE TRINITY	MARKS
FATHER	HOLY-HEAD
SON	LOVE-WORD
HOLY SPIRIT	CONVINCER

In the Divine Trinity, we have, of course:

The Father, who is the head (Holy),

The Son who is the Word and is the symbol of the love of the Father, (Jn 3:16, John 1:1);

and The Holy Spirit. Jesus said He will convict the world of sin, of justice and of judgment (John 16:8).

FAMILY TRINITY

FAMILY TRINITY	MARKS
FATHER	HOLY-HEAD
MOTHER	LOVE-WORD
CHILDREN	CONVINCERS

In the same way, there is a Family Trinity:

The Father: Head and Role Model

The Father is the head and supposed to be the role model, preaching by righteousness and justice exemplified, therefore holy.

The Mother: Love and Word of the Father

The Mother is love and the transmitter of the Father's word (vision) to the Children. We all know that she is affection and love personified. Classically, the Mother spends more time with the child (from child bearing and on) than the Father. And most of the time, she will convey the message of the Father to the Children such as:

"You know your father doesn't like that."

"Daddy told you not to do that."

"Remember what Dad said?"

This bears repeating: In the familial trinity, Mother is Love and the Word of the Father.

Children: The Convincers

Finally, the children are those who will convince anybody of the truth of your message. Somebody said that if you want to know if a pastor has integrity, while he is preaching, just look at his wife, and most of all, look at his children.

The attitude of the children, whether it is one of respect or scorn will tell you if this man is telling the truth or it's an act.

What are we saying?

The law of Trinity: Just as The Holy Spirit is the Convincer in the Divine Trinity, children are the Convincers in the Family Trinity. In other words: The real measure of your success is through the testimony of your children.

The question is: How do you get there?

Let us elaborate further on the family trinity.

FATHER: HEAD AND HOLY

Head or Leader: Where to?

The first attribute of a father is that he is appointed by God to be the Head of the Family, to lead the family into God's project for every marriage. The next question is: what project?

Let's read God's mission as stated to man.

First, after He created the first marriage, the Bible says in Genesis 1:

28God blessed them and said to them, "Be fruitful and increase in number; fill the earth and subdue it. Rule over the fish of the sea and the birds of the air and over every living creature that moves on the ground."

Then after the Flood, he gathered all four couples on earth at that time (i.e. Noah, his three sons with each his wife), and confirmed (Gen 9:1-3):

... "Be fruitful and increase in number and fill the earth. The fear and dread of you will fall upon all the beasts of the earth and all the birds of the air, upon every creature that moves along the ground, and upon all the fish of the sea; they are given into your hands. Everything that lives and moves will be food for you. Just as I gave you the green plants, I now give you everything

The two passages pretty much define the mission entrusted to the Head of families:

1.Be fruitful, increase in number and fill the earth.
To fulfill this mission, the obvious method is to:

Have children,
Raise them to get married and create their own families, from generation to generation,
Teach those children how to become, in turn, the fathers and mothers of tomorrow.

2.Subdue the rest of the Creation.

Considering how weak we are as humans when compared individually to the likes of lions, all the big cats, bears, elephants, whales, and sharks etc., this mission could obviously be achieved by what is best expressed by the famous French proverb: "L'Union fait la Force" or "Union is Power"; that is, society.

The head of the Family has, therefore, the duty to lead his family into to relating to and relying on the society.

3.Head of family's direction No 3:

In order to carry those two directions, it is the Head of the Family's responsibility to ensure there is Provision, starting with the physical provision for food, shelter, clothing, security, etc…

But, as said earlier, in chapter 1,

Man shall not live on bread alone, but on every word that comes from the mouth of God. (Matt 4:4)

It is therefore his responsibility to provide not only the physical, but also the Spiritual food of the Word of God at his family table daily!

So, mission No 3 for a family's Head is actually the most fundamental one, truly a condition single to none for existence:

It is to ensure his family has full life by having, not only the physical bread, but also the Spiritual Bread of life, staying in the presence of God through the feeding of the Word.

In conclusion, the mission of the man as head of the Family is to:

1: Keep his family in the presence of God through obedience to His Word.
2: Have children and raise them to be family leaders of tomorrow.
3: Lead his family to be good citizens.

MOTHER: THE WORD AND THE LOVE

The Mother, the Wife, must step in as the second in the family trinity and act like Jesus, the One second in the Divine Trinity, when he declared:

... for everything that I learned from ...Father I have made known to you. (John 15:15)

But the world must learn that I love ... Father and that I do exactly what ... Father has commanded me... (John 14:31)

This also requires that she accepts the recommendation of Paul that her attitude should be the same as that of Christ Jesus

who, being in very nature of God, did not consider equality with God something to be grasped, but made himself nothing, taking the very nature of a servant,... (Phil. 2 :6-7):

Women are by no means inferior to men; it is just a Divine order established by The Creator that the Man shall be the head for the good of the family; just as you submit to your boss at work, not because he or she is smarter or superior to you, but just because he or she has been established the boss. In the same way, you—woman—should accept the authority of your husband as a divine appointment to be the boss in the family enterprise!

Again, faithfulness in accepting, then transmitting of the father's instructions to the kids is the main key to family stability! Why?

Going back to Law No.4 and the fact that all divisions of God's authority have the same intra-rules, we raise the question:

What happens when the message from the top executives of a government is different or even contradicted by the lower executives?

Answer: Chaos!

Or, what happens when the message from the top executives of a company is different or even contradicted by the lower executives?

Answer: Chaos!

In the same way, unless the mother endorses and carries to the children the vision and the instructions of the Family's head (final instructions, in which, by the way, she may, have a big contribution, as the helper fit), chaos is guaranteed for the family, because, as Jesus put it in Mark 3:25: *If a house is divided against itself, that house cannot stand.*

We are not saying that husband and wife should never disagree on anything, no! It is impossible for two people to agree on everything! We are saying that in case of disagreement:

1.pray Pray and ask for God's guidance
2.Yes to Law No.1: Go to the Word
- -Check if any of the propositions is sinful.
- -If yes, what is the Bible recommending? Find it and obey!
- -If no sin, then,

3. Yes to Law No.5: Discuss the matter, remembering that:
    - You complement each other,
    - She sees what you cannot see, and vice-versa,
    - Find the compromise,
    - Asking yourself the eternal question: What if?
4. Finally, if there's still no compromise, as long as it's not sin, then yes to Law No.4:
    - Woman, please, just submit for the sake of the family, just as you probably do daily at your job,
    - Carry on his instructions as obeying the Lord, and the Lord will bless your family and your obedience.

THE POWER OF AGREEMENT.

Why? Because the Bible says in Matt 18:19

Again, I tell you that if two of you on earth agree about anything you ask for, it will be done for you by my Father in heaven

That is one of the most powerful promises of the Scriptures, with only one condition:

Agreement of both parties!

We have seen many couples whose projects fail and we have learned the hard way ourselves as a couple, when making the following mistake:

A Husband and his wife totally disagree on a matter, which is not a sin per se, they just have different opinions about a given project or issue. Each of them then camps on his/her position, yet they pray as a family time and time again. Of course, the project fails at the end. At that time, the one who was opposed says: "I told you so!!"

What a tragedy!! It is the other way around!!! The project failed because of only one reason: They failed, as a couple, to agree!
We have seen the reverse happen to us many a time: Real miracles happened for things which, by human logic and standards, were doomed to fail.

In those cases we found ourselves at an impasse. However, understanding the power of agreement, when the opposing person yielded, incredible things have happened! If only couples could understand the power of agreement!! Matt 18:19, *"...if two of you on earth agree "...*
is a powerful tool waiting for you as Husband and Wife. Take advantage of it and make it work for you!

So, please, husband and wife, by all means, find a compromise; and please mother, just carry faithfully your husband's message to the children, for true love's sake!! For the family's prosperity and blessing's sake!!

You and your family have untold blessings waiting in the air, on the mere condition that you are in agreement:

Agreement as a compromise!

Agreement even just to please your spouse!

Agreement even though all in you disagrees, but as long it's no sin, just agreement!

Agreement just to line-up your family and children under the umbrella of true blessings and true love!

It is only a trick of the enemy to make each of you hold his/her position for a matter which is not sinful, just to fulfill one's ego and have the pleasure to say:

I was right!

You were wrong!

I told you so!

THE LIMITS OF MOTHER-ALONE LOVE

It is only natural for any person to relate to Mother as love, and most women really are. The problem is to cross the line and believe mother's love is enough to raise a child. Someone declared:

The "relationship between crime and one-parent families"
is so strong that controlling the family configuration
(Father-Mother in a good marriage)
erases the relationships between race and crime
*and between low income and crime."(*3)*

One masterpiece of the enemy is to hail the virtues of single parenthood!

The best love you can give your child is the sacrifice of doing everything in your power to give him a stable family with husband and wife always striving to fulfill each his/her divine duties in the Family Trinity.

CHILDREN: THE CONVINCERS

As said in one famous popular Cameroon oldie song in pidgin (local slang):

".. Na whetty Papa di do Ooooh ..., pikin go do am Ooooh...!"

Translation:

"It is what Papa does that the children will do..."

What you are in the deepest, in the secret, will be transmitted to them. As true as they may resemble you physically or in character, in the spiritual realm also, they have your spiritual genes. Of course, this is true for the mother as well as for the father.

Most people will simply watch how your children are faring with whatever message you are teaching to see how serious you are.

We will always remember this incident that happened in our first year in the Lord: One Sunday afternoon of 1994, an angry woman burst into the House Church where we were worshipping and breaking bread, and created a big scandal.

Her son and her daughter, both in their late teens, had recently believed. They had been brought to the Church by Sister K. who was one of the Church leaders, and who had a problem: Her own children were simply bad boys in her neighborhood, and, of course did not walk with the Lord. Yet, Sister K. was so totally "consecrated" to the service of the Lord.

It was a dreadful sight: The woman was yelling, and screaming, and threatening in turn her own children, the Pastor and Sister K. She was holding a big stone in her right hand and a fistful of salt in the other. The angry mother violently threw salt over her children to "exorcise" them, saying: "You fools, how can this woman (Sister K.) blind you to bring you into that "Jesus" thing? Her own children don't believe it! They are liars, they are cheats, and they are armed-robbers in the neighborhood. She lied to you and you came in. Her own children don't believe her! You are fools to follow her…." She had previously vowed to harm our assembly Pastor and she had that big stone in her hand, ready to throw!

The whole scene was like it was straight out of a horror movie; all of us—the 20+ members of our house Church—trembling and fearing the worse, as one man, burst into praying in tongues. And sure enough, the Lord moved: Without any warning, the lady stopped yelling and walked out with the huge stone in her hand!

After taking a moment to recollect ourselves and with thanksgiving, we resumed the normal service… but those words of hers are still echoing in our hearts today.

Bottom line: All the consecration of our Sister K. was given a resounding zero mark before God and the World, due to the horrible testimony of her children.

CHILDREN ARE THE SIGN OF YOUR SUCCESS AND THE SYMBOL OF YOUR INTEGRITY

They only apply what they see and know of the real you.
Any sin of yours becomes immediately a seed which will grow and be exposed in their lives.

...For I, the LORD your God, am a jealous God, visiting the iniquity of the fathers upon the children to the third and fourth generations of those who hate Me, but showing mercy to thousands, to those who love Me and keep My commandments. (Ex 20:5-6)

Sons are a heritage from the LORD, children a reward from him. Like arrows in the hands of a warrior are sons born in one's youth. Blessed is the man whose quiver is full of them. They will not be put to shame when they contend with their enemies in the gate.
(Psalms 127:3-5)

My son, keep your father's commands and do not forsake your mother's teaching. (Proverbs 6:20)

A foolish son brings grief to his father and bitterness to the one who bore him. (Proverbs 17:25)

A foolish son is his father's ruin (Proverbs 19:13)

The Word of God confirms that children are the true mark of your success, the true mark of the success of your message, of your integrity. What is deep in you, either in integrity or in falsehood will be exposed in them at the maximum.

It is a spiritual law that they are immediately affected by your own sins, even the most secret ones.

The Example of Abraham and His Son Isaac

One example of this is Abraham. The Bible says that Abraham, when he went to Egypt, said to his wife:

"I know what a beautiful woman you are. When the Egyptians see you, they will say this is his wife. Then they will kill me, and they will let you live. Say you are my sister, so I will be treated well for your sake, and my life will be spared because of you". (Gen 12 v.11-12)

Later, in Genesis 20, he did it again. The Bible says in Genesis 20:2:

"There Abraham said of his wife Sarah: She is my sister!"

More than forty years later in Genesis 26, the Bible says in verse 7 that when the men of that place asked him about his wife, Isaac said:

"She is my sister!" because he was afraid to say "She is my wife". He thought that the men of that place might kill him on the count of Rebecca because she was beautiful.

The sin of the father was exactly repeated by the son in almost the same terms more than 40 years later.

The Example of David and his Household

Another frightening example: In 2 Samuel 11, the Bible says that David fell into sin. He committed adultery, killed the husband of the woman, and took her as his wife! Following that, in Chapter 12: God exposes his sins:

Immorality and murder.

And from 2 Samuel 13 on, the same sins were exposed all over his household and family:

His own son, Amnon, committed incest with Tamar who was David's daughter and therefore Amnon's sister;
As a result, Absalom killed his brother and one thing leading to another,
not only organized the first "Coup-d'Etat" in the Bible against his own father, with many people killed, but actually raped the ten wives of his own father!

Oh, the horror of sin from the head of the family!!

WHAT IS PARENTHOOD?

The Bible says:
And you, fathers, do not provoke your children to wrath, but bring them up in the training and admonition of the Lord. (Eph 6:4)

Train a child in the way he should go, and when he is old he will not turn from it. (Proverbs 22:6)

Using a sports analogy, that makes parents the trainers or coaches and children the athlete-trainees. Parenthood is coaching (training) children for the game of real life.

Scenario 1: Imagine a basketball coach teaching team A:
To dribble, do everything by the book, at the end, to shoot, not inside the ring, but exactly with one foot to the left of the ring!

Scenario 2: Another basketball coach teaching team B who:
Allows all kinds of contacts during his drill matches, so the players never get any faults, are never sanctioned during their preparation.

Question: Will any of those teams ever win the NBA championship?

Will team A ever win any championship with the current rules where the ball has to be set inside the ring for the basket to count?

Will team B ever make it beyond two quarters in any game without fouling out the entire roster?

Again, God expects parents to be coaches!

**LIFE IN SOCIETY IS THE REAL GAME;
FAMILY LIFE IS THE TRAINING SESSIONS!**

The children are the players; the parents the head coaches; and the school and education system are the assistant coaches.

	NBA	SOCIETY
Preparation	Training camp	Family
Teams players	NBA stars	Children
Head coaches	NBA head coaches	Father and mother
Coaching helpers	Deputy coaches	School/education system
REAL GAMES	CHAMPIONSHIP	LIFE IN SOCIETY
Method of preparation	Training per game rules	??

Life in the real world, in society, is the real game, with many rules. Allow us to summarize them into 3 general rules:

Rule 1: When you are:

Just complying with the laws and regulations,
With no violations, no fines, no tickets,
Paying your taxes correctly, etc…,

What you get:

You enjoy a good reputation, good friends around,
You are just ok,
Nobody is going to give you a special award for that.

Rule 2: When you

Excel in any field,
Or do anything good exceptionally well,
Develop special talents or skills,
Or display an uncharacteristically beautiful trait of good character to help a need or the society in general,

What you get:

Awards,
Prizes,
Medals,
Honorary distinctions,
Cups,
Champions rings,
Exceptional contracts,
Election to high positions,
Trust from the people, etc…

Rule 3: On the other side,

if you are found guilty of violating the laws of the land,

What you get:

Punishment is guaranteed, ranging
From a friendly warning and small fine,
To the death penalty, depending on the gravity of the violation.

In our seminars we always ask people:

"Cite one rule, one law so that, once you're brought before the judge and found guilty thereof, you'd get away without being condemned someway, somehow."

Answer: There could be grace, but in general, when you break the law, you pay with a fine, jail time, or even life in prison and/or sometimes execution.
There is punishment in the real game of life!

IN MANY FAMILIES, TRAINING RULES DON'T MATCH REAL-LIFE RULES

Unfortunately, in the process of training their children to real life, many parents have chosen to have home rules which are completely different from the ones in the real world, where they're going to send their children.

So, at home, a child can get away with any foul play, engage in bad behavior, violate any rule; and get away with anything bad in the name of "love", or with just a little slap on the wrist.

Whereas the Bible says in Proverbs 23:13,

"*Do not withhold discipline from a child. If you punish him with the rod, he will not die. Punish him with the rod to save his soul from death.*"

In Proverbs 13:24 the Bible adds:

"He who spares the rod hates his son,
but he who loves him is careful to discipline him."

As Paul says, t*he letter kills, and the Spirit gives life*. Therefore, understanding the spirit of the prescriptions, the concept of rod and the concept of a punishment can be adapted to each society according to the existing culture, rules and laws.

Yet, there are two major contradictions on this topic:

1)Many parents have set very lenient (and sometimes permissive) home rules for their children's education in the name of "love" and then they send them to the real game of social life where the rules are strict, with no mercy for violators.

2)Many legislators, through the blind generalization of the protection against child abuse, have literally "handcuffed" the good-willing parents in their ability and desire to train their children appropriately in family settings, and yet, on the other hand, the same legislators pass merciless laws to punish the flaws in resulting end products, when those juvenile turn criminals after being thrown into the real game of life. It is ok to protect children from abuse - we are all for that-, but a balance is needed in order to ensure that good-willing and truly loving parents still have the capacity to train their children properly for the real game of real life.

In our experience, the Lord has led us in raising our children, to duplicate the rules in real life.
On the good side:

If you (child) do good and consistently do right,
ok, you receive some kind of recognition.

Every time you do something exceptionally good
(good marks at school, good behavior, exceptional
generosity, something really outstanding),
you receive a gift and get a medal,
a special distinction from the family.

And, we make sure, as parents, to always keep our word as far as gifts are concerned.

Now, on the bad side, when you violate the rules, there's a scale of punishment used:

Starting with warnings (usually up to three);

After that, punishment ranges from grounding, through writing 200 times the sentence:

"I will no longer make this mistake again",
privileges frozen or lost,
to other kinds of punishment depending on the gravity of the "crime" committed.

And all this, while making sure the child understands:

This is training and correction for the real game of life: Real life in Society.
That punishment is therefore true love
by God's standards (Prov 13:24; Heb 12:7-8).

The father must be training the children, shaping boys into men, and the mother training the girls to become wives.

It's a big responsibility for the mother towards her daughters, in the way she behaves towards her husband; and it's a big responsibility for the husband, in the way he behaves with his wife: The children are watching; the children are feeling; the children are seeing.

THE 70-20-10 RULE

One great rule which is taught in many schools of communication applies particularly in the case of a family; that's the 70-20-10 rule, which states:

The impact of your message (what you are teaching your children) depends:

70% on what you are;
20% on what you do—your children are watching you;
And finally only 10% on what you tell them.

Ninety percent of what you impart to your children is without a word: Just being who you are and doing what you do!

You cannot be a smoker and tell your kids:

"Smoking is not good".

They will obey in your presence, while having in their hearts this famous French saying: "Cause toujours, mon gaillard!!" (Keep talking, dude!!)

They will hide it and do exactly as you do while waiting eagerly for the legal age to do it in the open, and there you go…! It goes the same way with every single bad habit of yours.

The truth is that all fathers and mothers are the first and true heroes to their children. It is also a spiritual law that everything you do is a seed into anything or anybody under your authority, beginning with your entire household and family.

That is the reason why the whole Creation fell into the hands of Satan with the fall of Adam: All creation had been submitted to Adam's authority (Gen 1:28); therefore by submitting to sin, that is, to the devil, he thereby submitted also everything under his authority (thus all his descendents-all Mankind) to the power of sin, therefore the enemy (Luke 4:5-7, Rom 5:19).

Fathers-Mothers: Just leading by example, 90% of the job is done!!!

Root change:

As a father, I will make sure that I am a real role model for my children, in all integrity:

Because my life is the greatest message they understand.

Because every sin that I commit, even in secret will be transmitted to these children; I cannot tell them "I love you" and yet live in sin (Rom13:9-10),

Because they will bear the punishment for the things that I've done;

Because I don't want to pollute my family with my personal sins.

As a mother I will particularly be careful in:

The way I treat my husband, the way I talk to him and about him, the way I honor him and respect him; I must be aware that I am indirectly teaching my children to do the same; and they will do just like me. And every sin that I have in my life, even the most secret will be transmitted to them.

The real measure of my success will be how much integrity I have transmitted to my children.

As parents, we are called to be coaches to our children for the game of real life in the Society: Success will come only if our family-training rules are relevant to the ones of the real life's game. The real measure of our success is how much of the fear of God we have transmitted to our children. The best way is to lead by example, and fear God ourselves, keeping His Word. This is the true love to our kids.

May the Lord bless you.

CHAPTER VII

YES TO LAW N°7: THE LAW OF EXALTATION

21

MARRIAGE IS THE PLACE FOR BROKENNESS!

The Bible says that pride is the cause for dissensions among men (Proverbs 13:10); this is more so true in Marriage.

Prof. Z.T. Fomum, our late Pastor, used to say it best:

"The problem with pride in a marriage is the following:
When you have a problem with your spouse, common sense should lead you to humiliate yourself in the secrecy of your intimacy, while it's just the two of you; one of you must simply bow and die to self in order to make peace!
If you so choose, the end result is that you are humiliated before only one person- actually before yourself, since the two of you are one!
This is where the devil steps in and blinds you, saying: 'No, no, and no! What are you doing? Don't make peace, don't bow! Keep your pride at all cost!'
And, pride makes you follow that advice, only to realize afterwards that you end up being humiliated before … the whole world, as your marital issues become public!"

Just turn your TV to divorce court shows and see how

couples can go against each other, and all that after having sworn eternal love, passion etc, to each other!

We often do not realize it, but imagine a President, or a Governor going public to declare in detail how bad the Vice-President or Lieutenant Governor of his own choosing is, or vice versa! In any place in the world, he himself would be dismissed from office for dire incompetence, because every single word against his office partner is a direct admission that he is himself unfit to rule!

The same goes with marriage!

The enemy deceives some people into thinking that bringing the weaknesses of their spouse to the public will make them look good or give them more respect in the public's eyes.

The truth is that the more a person slanders his/her spouse in public or vice-versa, for any reason at all, it's just the opposite: the lower he/she drops in the eyes of the audience, deep in everyone's heart. This is more so true for spiritual people, as the Word of God says in Eph 5:25-27:

Husbands, love your wives, just as Christ also loved the Church and gave Himself for her, that He might sanctify and cleanse her with the washing of water by the word, that He might present her to Himself a glorious Church, not having spot or wrinkle or any such thing, but that she should be holy and without blemish..

The Bible goes one step further to say that, not only should a man love his wife the way Christ loved the Church and gave (sacrificed) himself for her, but actually he is responsible for making sure there is no spot (sin) in her life!

That's the main reason why spouses need to humbly cooperate with the Lord!

GUARANTEED: THE WAY UP INTO PEOPLE'S TRUE ACCEPTANCE OF YOUR LEADERSHIP IS ACTUALLY THE WAY DOWN!

One thing about Wole Soyinka, the great Nigerian, Nobel Prize of literature in 1986, is the theory of "Tigritude" as they call it or "Tigerhood". He said something very simple, that we paraphrase like:

"A tiger does not have to proclaim his Tigerhood!"

Meaning: imagine we are downtown Indianapolis; suddenly we see a 400 lb tiger, out of its cage, padding into a meeting room where there are 50 people. We hardly expect him to come grab the microphone and say:

"Come on, watch me! Check Wikipedia and Google images and see for yourselves! I am a real tiger, folks: I'm dangerous!"

No, a tiger doesn't need to do that! A tiger just walks into the room, and you know where you should be!

The Law of Exaltation simply means that if you want to be respected by your spouse, you don't have to claim that you are the greatest. Don't ever claim your authority either as a wife or as a husband. The way of exaltation is described by many passages in the Bible:

"Not so with you is that. Whoever wants to become great among you must be your servant. And whoever wants to be first must be your slave." (Matt 20:26-27)

And in Matthew 23:11-12, the Bible says:

"The greatest among you will be your servant. For whoever exalts himself will be humbled, and whoever humbles himself will be exalted."

It is a spiritual law which applies more so among married couples.

This spiritual law of exaltation can be well illustrated by the old scale principle in Figure 1 and Figure 2:

On the left hand is your heart exaltation, and on the right the Lord's exaltation translated into the respect (crown) you truly receive from the hearts around you.

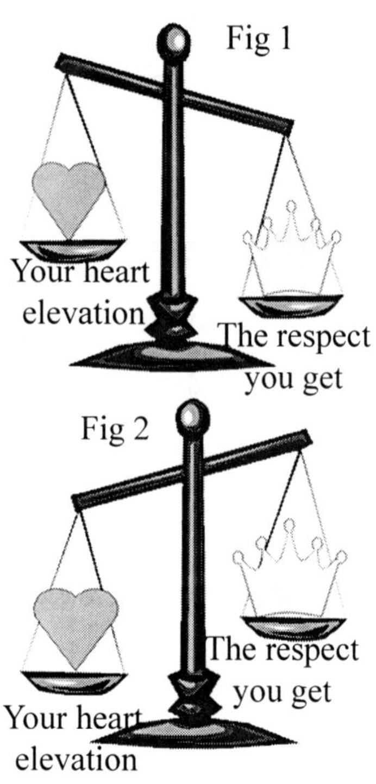

If one hand goes down, the other goes up and vice versa. A lowly heart attitude will yield great respect wherever you go, starting with your marriage, whereas a proud heart will yield only contempt deep inside people around you. They may show outward respect, honor and other convenience social marks of esteem as needed and required by the urge to be polite and/or to fit in the social mold, but deep inside, it's a different story.

ROGER

"When we were new arrivals to the US, my first employment was a delivery job for a company in Westminster, MD. Out of the tens of places I went in making deliveries, two names still ring in my memory: Mike and Jeff. These are the two humblest bosses I've ever seen! These two superintendants had numerous co-workers under them and yet, they always came and helped me unload while their workers were on the side watching; then, after a while, the workers would follow their lead. I mean, I remember always the respect that I had in my heart for these two people, and it was so obvious that they were highly respected among the workers too".

Family/marriage is the first and most important field for leadership, and that is the place where this biblical principle should be the most implemented!

WHAT MAKES MARITAL LEADERSHIP SO DELICATE?

As the Lord put it,

"*You know that the rulers of the Gentiles lord it over them, and their high officials exercise authority over them. Not so with you...." (Matt 20:25..)*

If a social authority gives an order, he or she has all the tools to oblige you to yield to them even if you do not want to obey:

The power of force (police and military for Governors and the like),
The power of money,
The power to break or end your social rise and ambitions,
The power to cut your society honors and rank (for bosses, schools and other institutions).

But in your marriage, what means do you have to bring your spouse to obedience?
The answer is right there in Ephesians 5:21-22 and verse 25:

Submit to one another out of reverence for Christ. Wives, submit to your husbands as to the Lord. Husbands, love your wives, just as Christ loved the Church and gave himself up for her.

How did Jesus love His bride, the Church?

"He was oppressed and afflicted, yet he did not open his mouth; he was led like a lamb to the slaughter, and as a sheep before her shearers is silent, so he did not open his mouth" (Isaiah 53:7)

Jesus accepted being unjustly accused and punished and did not open his mouth to accuse… the true guilty one who deserved that punishment: His bride, the Church.

"But he was pierced for our transgressions,
he was crushed for our iniquities;
the punishment that brought us peace was upon him,
and by his wounds we are healed." (Isaiah 53:5)

Could it be that this is the greatest secret to a glorious marriage?

That the perfect wife is the one who takes the low position, to submit to her husband for the Lord's sake; and the perfect husband the one who will go even lower to love and to own up without complaints or accusations to his wife's weaknesses?

...because love covers over a multitude of sins.
(1 Peter 4:8)

This explains why Marital Authority is more delicate:

It requires humility and lowliness simply because the other party must cooperate willingly to honor your leadership on one hand,

while on the other hand the two of you must reach a consensus for your authority to work, otherwise you operate out of the umbrella of mutual blessings (see Matt 18:19-20)

THE NAAMAN SYNDROME

The Bible relates the story of Naaman, a great Syrian general, in 2 Kings 5:

1 Now Naaman, commander of the army of the king of Syria, was a great and honorable man in the eyes of his master, because by him the LORD had given victory to Syria. He was also a mighty man of valor, but a leper. ...9 Then Naaman went with his horses and chariot, and he stood at the door of Elisha's house. 10 And Elisha sent a messenger to him, saying, "Go and wash in the Jordan seven times, and your flesh shall be restored to you, and you shall be clean." 11 But Naaman became furious, and went away and said, "Indeed, I said to myself, 'He will surely come out to me, and stand and call on the name of the LORD his God, and wave his hand over the place, and heal the leprosy.' 12 Are not the Abanah[a] and the Pharpar, the rivers of Damascus, better than all the waters of Israel? Could I not wash in them and be clean?" So he turned and went away in a rage. 13 And his servants came near and spoke to him, and said, "My father, if the prophet had told you to do something great, would you not have done it? How much more then, when he says to you, 'Wash, and be clean'?" 14 So he went down and dipped seven times in the Jordan, according to the saying of the man of God; and his flesh was restored like the flesh of a little child, and he was clean. 15 And he returned to the man of God, he and all his aides, and came and stood before him; and he said, "Indeed, now I know that there is no God in all the earth, except in Israel.

A few things about Naaman:

First, the amount of confidence he had in his abilities and his readiness to "buy" his blessing from God!

In fact, we tried to evaluate in today's value the amount Naaman was ready to pay for his healing; using today's stock prices for gold and silver and the weight estimated by the NIV bible:

NAAMAN'S GOLD AND SILVER AT TODAY'S QUOTES

	GOLD	SILVER
$ price/oz	$974.40	$17.62
Oz per Kg	32.15	32.15
No of Kg	69	340
Today's cost	$2,192,887.20	$192,604.22

TOTAL FOR GOLD/SILVER: $2,385,491.42

Naaman was willing to pay the equivalent of 2.385 million of today's US Dollars to be healed by God -1.39 billion CFA!

Secondly, his own vision and out-lay of God's healing process:

Naaman's idea of how to do it was that the Man of God would:

Come out to him,
Wave his hand over the sick parts of his body,
Heal him!

Instead, Elisha:

Did not show up personally,
Sent his servant to indicate God's prescription requiring that he, the great Naaman, remove his (certainly beautiful) General's uniform, and plunge himself, not once, not twice, not thrice, but …seven times in what he considered to be a dirty river!!

Thirdly, his attitude or pride facing the financially "cheap" (but honor-wise humiliating) cost for his cure!

In fact, in his mind he would have preferred to have his way, and one could imagine the scene of his honor parade upon his return to Damascus, passing in front of his fellow generals and before the King of Syria with heralds announcing loudly:

"Yet another mighty accomplishment of the great Naaman, just another glorious chapter to his excellent résumé: he just purchased his healing from the Mighty God of Israel for $2.3 million of our money! Hurrah, hurray! "

In short, God would have become just another luxury shop, with all the glory for Naaman!

And finally, his decision to humbly yield to God's prescription as the sole price to pay for final victory and blessing!

And he was on his way back to Damascus!! Furious!! Without healing!! And probably to his death!

Luckily he had great servants who helped him, saying in substance:

Great Naaman, you were ready to pay $2.3 million to be healed; How come you are ready to go back with your disease and with dishonor, when you can humble yourself here and now for free, get healed, and go back in all honors? Master, please do it!

And he did it, was healed, his eyes were opened to see the only true God, and finally he was elevated, not only before Man, but in time and eternity, after his miraculous conversion to the Living God!

What are we saying?

That many couples have what we call the Naaman Syndrome:

They are ready to pay "any price" for their marriage to work!

They are ready to invest the equivalent of Naaman's $2.3 Million in gifts, in counseling, in "marriage healing cruises", in a series of 21-day to 40-day fasts, in a series of prayer crusades and other "spiritual mighty deeds" for their marriage to work!

What do they all have in common with Naaman?

All the glory is theirs!!

Not to God!!

"You know what? This great marriage counselor cost us a fortune, but it was worth every bit of it: He advised me to offer this great gift to my spouse, and I did! And now we have a great marriage!"

God, who created marriage, declared the law of greatness:

"The greatest among you will be your servant. For whoever exalts himself will be humbled, and whoever humbles himself will be exalted." (Matt 23:11-12)

Could it be that the price for a glorious marriage is to accept the humility to be your spouse's servant from the heart?

No money, cruise, counselor fees or spiritual Mighty Deed needed! And just like for Naaman, the only cost is humility!!

For untold exaltation and happiness! For untold blessings and healings!

Let's make one thing clear: we are not against marriage counseling, gifts, spiritual and material investments into your marriage to make it better! All these things are great! And they work sometimes! Actually, they almost always work for some time!! For the simple reason that it is never the root-solution of the problem!

It's just a branch-cutting solution, just for a little time until the branches grow back!

The Bible says:

"Where there is strife, there is pride" (Prov 13:10); that is the root of marital problems, and the place to start permanent healing for a marriage.

Once the issue of pride is solved, the rest just falls into place and you are ready to be a servant that God will exalt in the eyes of your spouse and the whole world.

Spouses should be competing to serve each other. Those who apply this principle make the greatest couples.

Root Change :

Please, close your eyes for a moment and picture Jesus, the Christ, God Himself visiting His people!

Picture Him, the Perfect Bridegroom (of the Church, His Bride) and the greatest Leader in History, choosing to be born in a stable, among animals!

That's not all! He renounced His divine Nature to take the place of a servant in human form and accepted to die for the sins of His bride, The Church, in obedience to God (Phil 2:5-8)! In our humble opinion, that's the ultimate example of Humility!!

Now, please, read Philippians 2:9-11:

Therefore God exalted him to the highest place
and gave him the name that is above every name,
that at the name of Jesus every knee should bow,
in heaven and on earth and under the earth,
and every tongue acknowledge that Jesus Christ is Lord,
to the glory of God the Father.

That is the perfect application of the Law of Exaltation: if you take the position of a true servant of your spouse, you will be surprised to see how much God exalts you, not only in the eyes of your beloved half, but also in the eyes of everyone who knows you, from family, neighbors, friends, to social works partners, wherever you go!

Root Questions:

Are you the servant of your spouse?
Are you the servant of your children?
Do you ever claim your authority?

Yes to the 7th Law of A Glorious Marriage: Yes to the Law of Exaltation!

Yes, I will humble myself to be a servant to my spouse and my children, never claiming my authority, and God will exalt me in their hearts.

God bless you!

CONCLUSION

THE DOMINO PRINCIPLE

Back in the 1970's, ABC used to air a show featuring quite a few amazing domino masterpieces, with sometimes more than 10,000 chips, forming extraordinary figures. Once activated, all of them invariably turned into breathtaking combinations of artistic masterpieces of figures and shapes, popping out of a fantastic choreography of domino chips swirling around the set.

All of them always had an unforgettable finale with some kind of a jaw-dropping last gimmick which invariably made everyone "wow" in front of their TV set.

Also, all of them had one thing in common:

They all needed only one chip to cause all the rest to fall.

The 1977 hit movie "The Domino Principle" (*7) starring Gene Hackman, stated it best:

"Every organization has a central chip, so that, when that chip falls, the whole organization collapses."

That's the Domino Principle.

We re-baptize it as "The Marriage Principle" while we re-state it as follows:

For every human, any kind of success or achievement gravitates around a central chip. When that chip collapses, so does all the rest in that person's life. That central chip is marriage!

As we stated profusely through the previous chapters, the collapse of the family set-up is the beginning of the fall of any society. What we do not always see is that that collective collapse is the sum of individual collapses of people in that society!

And just as we said before, for each individual, failure in marriage brings to zero any achievement in the three main components of every human life: familial, social and spiritual.

Again, modern statistics prove beyond reasonable doubt that when a child is raised in a family home with father and mother in a good, healthy marriage, this alone will erase the majority of juvenile delinquency set-backs.

On the other hand, when a marriage fails, the children are usually the ones who pay the first and the heaviest price, as their shattered lives are usually the true mark for their parents' familial, social and spiritual achievements.

One important note: We are not saying that when marriage fails, a person cannot have success per se!

Not at all! Mighty things can really be achieved! Trophies, prizes and awards can be won! And spiritual ministries can each expand to become a worldwide phenomenon! But as Billy Dee Williams said it so well to Diana Ross in "Mahogany", the 1975 hit movie:

"Success is nothing, nothing...
without someone you love to share it with!"

(Mahogany (1975) Motown Productions, Nikor Productions, Paramount)

Just think about this: How many political, artistic and humongous sports careers, how many anointed Ministries have come to a halt lately, just because of one scandal or infidelity bringing a marriage to a collapse? And we are talking about people whose achievements sometimes are still in the History books and will probably stay there for a long time!

But all that is reduced to zero in people's eyes, as multi- million dollar endorsements and supports of all kinds (political, social, sports and spiritual) are simply wiped out from the table under public pressure, as if the whole world were merely saying loud and clear:
"All you've achieved in the past has now become zero in the eyes of the society, for only one reason: You have failed in your marriage!"

Yet, all this is nothing in comparison to seeing one's lifetime achievements for the Lord tested on That Day through the fire of God's appraisal, with the final, Eternity mark:

No gold, No silver, No precious stones,
Rather, wood, hay and straw... (1 Cor 3:12)
Cause: failed marriage (1 Tim 3:5, 1 Tim 5:8; 1 Cor 13:1)

Please, don't let it happen to you! Don't let the enemy rejoice over you! Protect the most important chip in the domino setting of your life: Protect your marriage!

Here is a good place to start:
Say Yes to the 7 Laws of a Glorious Marriage!

And may the Lord who created marriage bless you richly!

REFERENCES

(*1)The Bible: various translations were used and quoted.

(*2) A Successful Marriage: The Husband's Making , by Z.T. Fomum, CPH productions, 2007

(*3) The Fall of Marital Family Stability and the Rise of Juvenile Delinquency -A publication by Lynn D. Wardle, 2008

(*4) Dept. Of health and Human Servs. Admin. For families & children, Health Marriage Initiative, Benefits Of Healthy Marriages For Children And Youth: 2006 report available at http://www.acfhh s.gov/healthymarriage/about/mission.html

(*5) The Power Of Your Words –by Don Gosset and E. W. Kenyon, published by Whitaker House, 1977

(*6) The Ministry of Fasting – by Z.T. Fomum, CPH productions, 1991

(*7) The Domino Principle by Stanley Kramer 1977, Associated General Films & ITC, AVCO Embassy Pictures, Plan Film)

TABLE OF CONTENT

CPSIA information can be obtained at www.ICGtesting.com
Printed in the USA
BVOW030322250413

319049BV00001B/1/P